RECENT TREND IN EDUCATIONAL RESEARCH

RECENT TREND IN EDUCATIONAL RESEARCH

Edited by

Dr. D.Sivakumar

Associate Professor

Department of Education

Dr. Sivanthi Aditanar College of Education

Tiruchendur, Tamil Nadu

(INDIA)

D P H

DISCOVERY PUBLISHING HOUSE PVT. LTD.

NEW DELHI-110 002

Published by:

Tilak Wasan

DISCOVERY PUBLISHING HOUSE PVT. LTD.

4383/4B, Ansari Road, Darya Ganj

New Delhi - 110 002 (India)

Phone : +91-11-23279245, 43596064-65

Fax : +91-11-23253475

E-mail : discoverypublishinghouse@gmail.com

sales@discoverypublishinggroup.com

website : www.discoverypublishinggroup.com

***First Edition:* 2015**

ISBN: 978-93-5056-741-8

Recent Trend in Educational Research

Printed at:

Infinity Imaging Systems

Delhi

Preface

Education has purpose. A role to play in shaping our future generation and achieving the dream, the goal humankind has set for himself, *i.e.*, to continuously excel and constantly achieving the better and satisfying the unfailing curiosity to know the outer universe and the inner of own consciousness. All knowledge is constantly gathered, experimented and applied to the welfare of humankind. And this mechanism of transferring knowledge and skills to the next generation is our system of education or education itself. As teachers, educationists, parents, administers, mentors we must all continuously explore how our methodologies can be successful to educate our children and help them to germinate with values and wisdom. With the development of technology and changing social demands our mechanism *i.e.*, education need to be contemplated and perpetually evolved to meet the new challenges, our daily life presents.

Across the globe, in small as well as big countries, in developed, developing and undeveloped countries, among policy-makers, researchers, education managers and teachers, one overriding concern has been to improve the quality of the schooling experience their young citizens are exposed to. Future citizens face a challenging and uncertain future. All children require access to high quality education. Building a high-quality education system relevant to 21st century social and economic realities has therefore become a top policy issue. This in turn has focused attention on a range of issues related to the recruitment, selection, preparation and deployment of teachers. Recognizing the above and the basic fact that the universities and colleges have to perform multiple roles, like creating new knowledge, acquiring new capabilities and producing an intelligent human resource and extension activities so as to balance both the need and the demand.

Research is endless for knowledge or unending search for truth. It is rather a speech that provides knowledge for solution of problems in the field of education. So it is the need of the day to carry research in every field and more see in the field of education progress in any field is directly linked with the research in it. To take in hand research work is one of the most valuable services related towards mankind. It is enhances the efficiency of all agencies engaged in the welfare of man.

In this book, an effort has been made to put together a selection of articles related to education. The coming times will show whether the reforms initiated now will create a revolution in education. There is a sincere attempt to place before the readers a wide selection of views and opinions related to the ongoing and projected reforms and the future of education in our nation. We express our deep respect and gratitude for the contributors, because of whom this could be made possible.

In my view the main reason to publish the edited book entitled: '*Recent Trend in Educational Research*' is to say something new and to add value to what has already been said essentially this book attempts to round out and contemporize each topic without adding unnecessary detail or complexity. It takes a broader and deeper look at the various research paradigms, designs, tools, and statistical technique to allow researchers to better respond to the research demands of today's world. I maintain my belief that this text short be short, yet provide all the essential with enough breath and depth to develop a well rounded researcher.

Editor

Contents

Page 1-9

Recent Trend in Educational Research
Edited by: **Dr. D. Sivakumar**
Edition: **2015**
ISBN: 978-93-5056-741-8
Published by: **Discovery Publishing House Pvt. Ltd., New Delhi (India)**

1

Professional Development of College Teachers - Does it Enhance Teaching Competency?

Dr. S. Francisca

INTRODUCTION

Professional development is an ongoing process of enhancement and maintenance of the skills, competencies and knowledge for both personal development and career advancement also to accommodate the impacts of the rapidly changing social, economic and technological advancements. Since Professional development (PD) is a support given to individuals to enhance their career prospects, to do their job better it is an important mechanism in any field of work and is equally important for educators. Professional development for teachers refers to the in-service training provided to teachers to up-grade their content knowledge and pedagogical skills from a wide variety of learning opportunities encountered in their career path. The terms staff development, in-service, and professional development are often used interchangeably (J. David Cooper). Professional development encompasses all types of facilitated learning opportunities, professional membership, reading, summer sessions, sabbaticals, self-directed private study, relevant

Associate Professor, St. Ignatius College of Education, Palayamkottai.

voluntary work, conventions, workshops, conferences and informal learning opportunities situated in practice.

Need for Professional Development for College Teachers

Teaching competence in higher education refers to the right way of conveying units of knowledge, application, and skills to students. Large number of instructional and other related activities performed by the teacher in the classroom setting involves effective organization of these activities which would involve certain knowledge, attitudes and skills. It includes knowledge of content, processes, methods and means of conveying the content. Even experienced teachers confront great challenges each year, including changes in subject content, new instructional methods, advances in technology, changed laws and procedures, and student learning needs. Educators who do not experience effective professional development do not improve their skills, and student learning suffers. (Hayes Miztell, 2010). In the changing environment of higher education institutions characterized by competitive global educational market, the importance of professional development has been recognized as essential to support new approaches to learning and teaching and the changing needs of institutions (Blandford, 2001). Since the professional development is the key mechanism for teacher improvement directed towards student learning, the professional development activities for the college teachers is indispensable in assuring the quality in higher education system. The academic staff experiences presented aim principally at improving the academic qualifications of higher education teachers in order to upgrade their level of training and research. The ability of staff to assure excellence in a given field – mainly through advanced post-graduate qualifications – is crucial if a higher education institution is to award a degree or diploma in that discipline.(UNESCO, 1994). Staff development is also a commitment for all staff to improve their levels of skills knowledge to improve the quality of workforce productivity and staff satisfaction. Professional development facilitates personnel and professional development for individuals and groups, enabling them to achieve their potential and contribute to the provision of excellence in teaching and research. In regard to the university setting, the importance of staff development in increasing effectiveness in the university, it was argued that staff development facilitates personnel and professional development for individuals and groups, enabling them to achieve their potential and contribute to the provision of excellence in teaching and research in the university (University of Cambridge, 2006). Effective professional development is essential to support new approaches to learning and teaching and meeting the changing needs of institutions as to maintain the high educational standards.

Statement of the Problem

Professional development is supposed to enhance those knowledge and skills and broaden the attitude of the teachers which would attenuate the teaching competency. So this study supposes that the teaching competency would enhance through professional development activities.

Operational Definitions

(i) *Teaching competency:* Teaching competency is one or more abilities of a teacher to produce agreed upon educational effects. In the present study 'teaching competency', the investigator means competencies such as: subject mastery, motivation and introduction, use of teaching aids, communication, classroom management and providing emotional support.

(ii) *Professional development:* Professional development is a process of developing one's knowledge, skills and competencies required in a profession so as to meet the contemporary and future demands of that particular profession. In this present study by 'professional development' the investigator means the professional development activities undertaken by the college teachers such as: attending the refresher courses, workshops, conferences, seminars etc.

(iii) *College teachers:* The teachers working in the institutes of higher learning are meant as college teachers. The teachers of higher education or beyond the school education are called college teachers.

Methodology

To solve the present problem the investigator has employed descriptive method using survey as a technique. The investigator had used self-developed and validated Teaching Competency Scale and Professional Development checklist. The professional development checklist is formulated on the basis of the guidelines provided by the UGC on the various staff development activities that can be initiated by teachers for professional development. It is self-reported checklist by the teachers and containing 14 items such as attended conferences/ workshops/seminars and refresher courses, short-term courses, long-term courses, organizing conferences, paper presentations etc., and many subdivisions under each item. For every item checked scoring was done. A sample of 310 teachers drawn through simple random sampling technique from various arts and science, and teacher education colleges in Kanyakumari district were requested to fill in the checklist. The teaching competency Scale is a student reported assessment about their teachers under various dimensions of teacher competency. A sample of 1550 students participated in this survey assessing the competencies of their teachers to whom the professional development checklist was administered, wherein for every teacher five students completed the teaching competency scale. Data had been analyzed calculating mean, SD, 't' test and Karl Pearson's product moment correlation.

Data Analysis

Null Hypothesis – 1

There is no significant correlation between Professional Development and teaching competency of college teachers.

Table 1.1: Correlation between Professional Development and Teaching Competency of College Teachers

Total Sample	Count	'r' value	Table Value	Result
College teachers	310	0.341	0.088	S

Null Hypothesis – 2

There is no significant difference between teachers in Professional Development with reference to background variables.

Table 1.2: Difference between Teachers in Professional Development with Reference to Background Variables

Variables	Categories	Count	Mean	SD	t-value	Result
Gender	Male	120	52.44	12.89	3.09	significant
	Female	190	48.46	7.26		
Type of Institution	Affiliated	218	49.67	9.55	0.84	Not significant
	Autonomous	92	50.78	11.01		
Domicile (Institution)	Rural	179	49.63	8.59	0.73	Not significant
	Urban	131	50.51	11.67		

Null Hypothesis – 3

There is no significant difference between teachers in teaching competency and its dimensions with reference to Gender.

Table 1.3: Difference between Teachers in Teaching Competency with Reference to Gender

Dimension	Variable	Count	Mean	SD	't'-value	Result
Subject Mastery	Male	120	48.50	11.56	1.99	significant
	Female	190	50.95	8.77		
Motivation and Introduction	Male	120	48.65	11.36	1.79	Not significant
	Female	190	50.85	8.96		
Use of Methods and Skills	Male	120	49.45	10.69	0.75	Not significant
	Female	190	50.35	9.55		
Communication	Male	120	49.51	10.32	0.68	Not significant
	Female	190	50.31	9.81		
Classroom Management	Male	120	48.87	10.67	1.54	Not significant
	Female	190	50.71	9.51		
Emotional Support	Male	120	48.74	10.50	1.74	Not significant
	Female	190	50.80	9.62		
Total Teaching Competency	Male	120	48.86	10.42	1.58	Not significant
	Female	190	50.72	9.68		

(At 5% level of significance the table value of 't' is 1.96)

Null Hypothesis – 4

There is no significant difference between teachers in teaching competency and its dimensions with reference to Type of Institution.

Table 1.4: Difference between Teachers in Teaching Competency with Reference to Type of Institution

Dimension	Variable	Count	Mean	SD	t-value	Result
Subject Mastery	Affiliated	218	50.79	9.52	2.04	Significant
	Autonomous	92	48.13	10.89		
Motivation and Introduction	Affiliated	218	51.17	9.46	3.06	Significant
	Autonomous	92	47.22	10.73		
Use of Methods and Skills	Affiliated	218	50.79	10.19	2.25	Significant
	Autonomous	92	48.12	9.32		
Communication	Affiliated	218	51.04	9.69	2.77	Significant
	Autonomous	92	47.54	10.34		
Classroom Management	Affiliated	218	50.03	9.86	1.69	Not significant
	Autonomous	92	48.51	10.23		
Emotional Support	Affiliated	218	50.93	9.74	2.50	Significant
	Autonomous	92	47.78	10.32		
Total	Affiliated	218	51.11	9.50	2.92	Significant
	Autonomous	92	47.36	10.68		

(At 5% level of significance the table value of 't' is 1.96)

Null Hypothesis – 5

There is no significant difference between teachers in teaching competency and its dimensions with reference to Domicile.

Table 1.5: Difference between Teachers in Teaching Competency with Reference to Domicile

Dimension	Variable	Count	Mean	SD	t-value	Result
Subject Mastery	Rural	179	50.56	9.59	1.14	Not significant
	Urban	131	49.23	10.52		
Motivation and Introduction	Rural	179	51.11	9.40	2.25	Significant
	Urban	131	48.49	10.62		
Use of Methods and Skills	Rural	179	50.91	9.95	1.89	Not significant
	Urban	131	48.75	9.97		
Communication	Rural	179	51.13	9.95	2.35	Significant
	Urban	131	48.45	9.90		
Classroom Management	Rural	179	50.78	9.83	1.61	Not significant
	Urban	131	48.93	10.16		
Emotional Support	Rural	179	51.20	9.78	2.48	Significant
	Urban	131	48.36	10.10		
Total	Rural	179	51.19	9.34	2.42	Significant
	Urban	131	48.37	10.66		

(At 5% level of significance the table value of 't' is 1.96)

Findings and Discussions

From Table 1.1 it is evident that there is positive correlation between the professional development and teaching competency which indicates that the professional development initiatives certainly improve the skills and attitudes of teaching competency. Much of research supports this relationship between professional development and teaching competency, whereas Guskey, 2002 proposes a model which portrays the temporal sequence of events from professional development experiences to enduring change in teachers' attitudes and perceptions. A large amount of funding is being disseminated by the higher education bodies UGC to conduct seminars, conferences, workshops and refresher courses through its academic staff colleges as a part of its faculty development agenda. But all these activities aimed at the professional enhancement must be carefully tailored to the growing challenges faced by the higher education sector. To be effective, professional development should be based on curricular and instructional strategies that have a high probability of affecting student learning – and, just as important, students' ability to learn (Joyce and Showers, 2002). Professional development of teachers and teacher educators and teacher education curriculum for assessment and evaluation for learning and pedagogy are important areas of designing professional development initiatives. (UGC, 12th FYI, 2012)

Analyzing professional development with reference to the background variables gender, type of institution and domicile from Table 1.2, it is evident that there exists significant difference only in case of gender. This may be attributed to the chances of availing the professional activities accessible by male faculty are more than their female counterparts. Also a study conducted by (Lauri Hyers *et al.* 2012) indicate the existence of disparities in the Professional Development Interactions of University Faculty as a Function of Gender and Ethnic Under-representation.

From Table 1.3, 1.4, 1.5 the teaching competency of the teachers under various dimensions with reference to the background variables, indicate that teaching competency as a whole as well as in its various dimensions does not significantly differ with reference to gender except for subject mastery. Also it is evident that there exists significant differences in the teaching competency and its dimensions except for classroom management between the teachers of the affiliated and autonomous colleges. Similarly the teaching competency is found to differ depending upon the domicile, the location of the institution whether situated in urban or rural locale, but in few dimensions like subject mastery, Use of methods and classroom management there are no significant differences.

Conclusion

If the goal of education reform is to improve student performance through changes in teaching practices, and if changes in teaching practices are likely to result only from high-quality professional development, (Harwell, 2003) the professional development should be characterized by high-quality standards. Higher education institutions can design to put in place appropriate professional development strategies to support all faculty and encourage involvement in the development and implementation of university-wide policies and strategies because effective staff development is essential to support new approaches to learning and teaching, and meeting the changing needs of the higher educational sector.

REFERENCES

Blandford, S. (2001). Professional Development in Schools. In: Early Development for Teachers, edited by F. Bank and S. A. Mayes. London: David Fulton Publishers, pp. 9-28.

Joyce, B., and Showers, B. (2002). Student Achievement through Staff Development. Alexandria, Virginia: Association for Supervision and Curriculum Development.

David J. Cooper, Current Research, Professional Development: An Effective Research based Model, Houghton Mifflin Harcourt retrieved from http://www.greatsource.com/GreatSource/pdf/ProfessionalDevelopmentResearch.pdf on 6.01.2012.

Hyers, Lauri L.; Syphan, Janet; Cochran, Kelly; Brown, Timothy. (2012). Disparities in the Professional Development Interactions of

University Faculty as a Function of Gender and Ethnic Under Representation. *Journal of Faculty Development*, v26 n1 p. 18-28 Jan. 2012.

UNESCO, 1994. Higher Education Staff Development :Directions for 21st century. Published in 1994 by the United Nations Educational, Scientific and Cultural Organization 7, place de Fontenoy, 75352 Paris 07 SP retrieved from http://www.usc.es/ceta/recursos/documentos/barnes.pdf on 5.01.2012

Page 10-16

Recent Trend in Educational Research
Edited by: **Dr. D. Sivakumar**
Edition: **2015**
ISBN: 978-93-5056-741-8
Published by: **Discovery Publishing House Pvt. Ltd., New Delhi (India)**

2

Effectiveness of Trainer Guided Module for Developing E-teaching Competencies among B.ED. Trainees

A.Kanaharaj[1] and **Dr. S. Malathi**[2]

INTRODUCTION

Online Education involves online teaching and online learning along with the various administrative and strategic measures needed to support teaching and learning in an Internet environment. Online Teaching involves using online tools to support student learning. Online Teachers are the new generation of teachers who will work in an Internet environment in both regular and virtual classroom situations. They will build new concepts of working in time and space. Online teachers collaborate, build and discover new learning communities and explore resources as they interact with information, materials and ideas with their students and colleagues. They have to mediate computer Conferencing and should know how make use of Bulletin Boards and e-mails to facilitate online learning. They are expected to play roles of process facilitator, adviser, Assessor, Researcher, Content

1. Research Scholar, Department of Education, Alagappa University, Karaikudi.
2. Asst.Professor in.Education, DDE, Alagappa University, Karaikudi.

Facilitator, Technologist, Designer, Manager and Administrator in an online environment. Online teachers should focus not only on the technical capacities and functions of IT materials and activities, but must attempt to understand more fully about how their e-learners perceive the learning environment.

Objectives

1. To identify E-teaching competencies.
2. To develop a trainer guided module for developing E-teaching Competencies among B.Ed. Trainees.
3. To measure the effectiveness of trained guided module for developing E-teaching competencies among B.Ed. Trainees.

Hypotheses

1. There is no significant difference between the control and experimental groups of B.Ed. teacher trainees in their gain scores.
2. There is no significant difference between control and experimental groups of B.Ed. teacher trainees in their scores in handling web browsers, creating user accounts and communicating through e-mails.
3. There is no significant difference between pre-test and post-test scores of control and experimental groups of B.Ed. teacher trainees.

Methodology

The investigators employed two equivalent group experimental designs for the study. As the experimental research is a common approach followed in finding out effectiveness of treatment, the investigators followed experimental research for finding out the effectiveness of trainer guided module for developing e-teaching competencies among the students undergoing B.Ed. course. The research design chosen for experimental research has four important phases.

Equivalent Group Formation

Twenty Six B.Ed. trainees from IGNOU Study Centre, Trivandrum have been selected for the study. An advantage of selecting trainees undergoing B.Ed. from IGNOU is that all are in-service teachers having a minimum of two years teaching experience in various recognized schools in different part of the country. A pre-test has been conducted during the selection process for selecting in-service teacher trainees for both control and experimental groups. Utmost care has been taken to see that the there is no mean significance difference between these groups in the pre-test scores.

Tools Deployed

1. A trainer guided module was developed and validated by the investigators for training the experimental groups.
2. Investigators constructed achievement test for evaluating e-teaching competencies. The tool was duly validated by the investigators.

Conducting Experiment

The investigators developed one module for e-teaching competencies as a trainer guided module to train the in-service teacher trainees. The trainer guided module has the wider coverage of lab activities with computer system for developing competencies on the following areas.

- Competency to use various web browsers.
- Competency to create user account in terms of user id and password.
- Competency to send, receive and read e-mails.

The experimental group has 13 in-service teacher trainees. They have been taken to computer laboratory and trained them using trainer guided module. Each student was provided with independent computer system with high speed internet connectivity. During the training phase using trainer guided module, proper care was taken to ensure that each student acquired competency to the level of expectations on how to use various web browsers with the help of which they would be able to connect internet world and how to create user account for each student by creating user id and password. If there exists already a user of same name, hints were provided to the students to rename user id that matched the entities of his or her interest. The students were trained on how to code password and minimum standards to be followed in coining the password. The students were trained on one month as the classes were conducted on weak ends.

The control group has the sample size of 13 and the mean score obtained by them in the pre test do not vary much with the mean score obtained by the trainees belonging to experimental group. These students were taken to regular class room and were taught in the traditional way using power point and other teaching aids on the above topics pertaining to various web browsers and how to use them for gaining access to internet services. The trainees were taught on how to create user account using user id and password and then how to communicate with the others by e-mails.

Statistical Techniques Employed

Following statistical analysis were performed in the study.

1. Mean.
2. Standard Deviation.
3. T-test.

Hypothesis Testing

Table 2.1: Difference between Control and Experimental Group of in-service B.Ed. Teacher Trainees in their Gain Score

Group	Mean	Standard Deviation	Calculated 't' value	Remark at 5% Level
Control group	6.21	2.3	3.99	**Significant
Experimental group	9.44	1.8		

(At 5% level of significance the table value of t is 2.064)

The calculated t value is 3.99 which is greater than the table value of t at 5 per cent (2.064). Therefore null hypothesis is rejected. It is inferred from Table 2.1 that there is a significant difference between the gain scores in the control and experimental group. There is a significant difference between the control and experimental groups of B.Ed. teacher trainees in their gain scores.

The calculated t value for the scores obtained in handling web browsers is 4.14 which is greater than the table t value for degree of freedom 24 (2.064). Similar inference is observed in creating user account and e-mail communications.

Table 2.2: Difference between Control and Experimental Group of in-service B.Ed. Teacher Trainees in their Gain score in Handling web Browsers, Creating user Accounts and Communications through E-mails

Competencies	Control Group		Experimental Group		Calculated 't' value	Remarks at 5% Level
	Mead	SD	Mean	SD		
Handling of Web Browsers	3.22	1.30	5.21	1.02	4.14	**Significant
Creating User Account	1.77	1.10	3.23	1.01	3.52	**Significant
E-mail Communication	1.52	1.12	2.93	1.02	3.36	**Significant

(At 5% level of significance the table value of t is 2.064)

Therefore the null hypothesis is rejected. Hence There is a significant difference between control and experimental groups of B.Ed. teacher trainees in their scores in using web browsers, creating user accounts and communicating through e-mails.

Table 2.3: Difference between Pre-test and Post-test Scores of Control and Experimental Group of in-service B.Ed. Teacher Trainees

Group/ Test	Control Group		Experimental Group		Calculated 't'-Value	Remarks at 5% Level
	Mean	SD	Mean	SD		
Pre-test	7.23	2.12	7.27	2.06	0.29	Not significant
Post-test	13.41	2.01	18.83	1.73	6.84	**Significant

(At 5% level of significance the table value of t is 2.064 for df=24)

It is inferred from Table 2.3 that there is no difference between the pre-test scores of experimental and control groups of B.Ed. teacher trainees where as there calculated t value of post-test scores between the control and the experimental group is 6.84 which is greater than the table value corresponding to the 'df value' of 24. The null hypothesis is rejected. Hence there is a significant difference between post-test scores of control and experimental groups of B.Ed. teacher trainees.

Major Findings

- There was a significant difference between the control and experimental groups of B.Ed. teacher trainees in their gain scores. Experimental group students were better than the control group students as far as their gain scores were concerned.
- There was a significant difference between control and experimental groups of B.Ed. teacher trainees in their gain scores in handling web browsers, creating user accounts and communicating through e-mails. Experimental group teacher trainees have scored better gain scores than the teacher trainees belonging to control group in handling web browsers, creating user accounts and communicating through e-mails.
- There was no significant difference between pre-test gain scores of control group and experimental groups of students of B.Ed. teacher trainees whereas there was a significant difference between post-test scores of control and experimental groups of B.Ed. teacher trainees. Experimental group was able to get a higher gain score that the control group.

Interpretation

The calculated t value shows that there is significant difference in between the control and experimental groups of B.Ed. teacher trainees in their gain scores. Experimental group students were better than the control group students as far as their gain scores were concerned. It is because of the effect of effective use of trainer guided module in developing e-teaching skills among the teacher trainees.

Conclusion

Gilly Salmon defines the most essential competencies required for an online teachers under the 5 categories such as: Understanding online environments, Technical Competencies, Online Communication Competencies, Content Expertise. An attempt has been made to develop trainer guided modules covering all the above categories. Initially one module has been developed to train the teacher trainees on understanding online environment with a certain set of activities. The Module has been validated and used for developing e-teaching competencies to B.Ed. teacher trainees. The module was found to be more effective in developing e-teaching competencies among the B.Ed. trainees.

REFERENCES

Gilly Salmon: E-moderating – The Key to Teaching and Learning online TYLOR and Francis Book Ltd., Oxon 2008.

R. A. Sharma: Basic Experimental Designs in Educational and Psychological Research Surya Publication, Meerut (2006).

A. Rajathi and P. Chandran: SPSS for you MJP Publishers, Trichy 2010.

C. R. Kothari: Research Methodology Methods and Techniques: New Age International Publications 2008.

Dr. Lokanandha Reddy, R. Ramar, L. Ponnambalam 'Effectiveness of Comprehensive Social Skill Strategy in Overcoming Social Skill Deficiency' RRE, Vol. 10 , No. 04, pp. 5-8.

K. Thiyagu and I. Muthuchamy "Effectiveness of E-content in Learning Mathematics among Secondary Teacher Trainees" RRE Vol. 10 No. 04 p. 9-12.

Page 17-22
Recent Trend in Educational Research
***Edited by:* Dr. D. Sivakumar**
***Edition:* 2015**
ISBN: 978-93-5056-741-8
***Published by:* Discovery Publishing House Pvt. Ltd., New Delhi (India)**

3

Correlates of Attitude and Professional Ethics Towards Teaching Profession for Secondary Level Teachers

M. Venmani

INTRODUCTION

Teacher education in our country has to face the challenge of producing teachers for a new society. However in order to meet the challenge successfully, it is necessary to improve the quality to teacher educators. Teaching is a lifetime profession and also due to the rapid explosion of knowledge and scientific inventions, the attitude of teachers towards their profession is changing rapidly. 'Good education requires good teachers'. Professional ethics are essential to become a good teacher. Teachers are duly licensed professionals who possess dignity and reputation with high moral values as well as technical and professional competence in the practice of their noble profession and they strictly adhere to observe, and practice this set of ethical and moral principles, standards, and values.

Attitude Towards Teaching Profession

Teaching is a profession, which lays the foundation for preparing the individual for all other profession. S. Kannan

Ph.D., Research Scholar, N.K.T. National College of Education for Women, Triplicane, Chennai - 600 005.

and N. Subramanian (2004) in their study. 'Teacher Attitude towards Teaching' said that "Attitude is sum total of man's imagination and feelings, prejudice or bias, preconceived notions about a specific topic. It is admittedly a subjective and professional affair." It affects \\\perception, judgment and other cognitive process of a teacher. The Kothari Commission on Education (1964-66) has emphasized the role of school and the teacher in shaping the future of the nation. The shape will undoubtedly depend on what goes in the classroom and how it goes on. This places a greater responsibility on the shoulders of the teacher as nation builders.

According to Challenges of Education document (1985), teachers have special responsibilities in every society and the way they are discharged sets the tone for education of the young. They have the potential to mould the tender minds of students so that they become good citizens and good human beings. But the perception today is that, this is not happening. The reasons are many and varied. Every profession is supposed to have an accepted code of ethics specific to the nature of the profession. Teacher like other professionals, have the similar responsibility, not only to the individual but also to the society is a conscious and learned member. The National Policy on Education, (1986) places complete trust in the teaching community. It also emphasizes the need for preparation of a code of Professional Ethics for Teachers to ensure that teachers perform their duties in accordance with acceptable norms. It is expected that the code of professional ethics, is observed sincerely by the teachers shall enhance their commitment to the profession on one hand and improve their effectiveness on the other.

Professional Ethics for Teaching Profession

Parents handover the future of their children to the teacher. So a teacher should carry out the expectations of home society, community and nation. Teaching is the most responsible profession than any other profession. A teacher is the topmost person in the professional pyramid because the teacher makes all other professional.

- Commitment to the teaching profession.

- Commitment to students.
- Commitment to colleagues.
- Commitment to parents.
- Commitment to community.
- Commitment to self and management.

Objectives of the Study

1. To find out the relationship between Attitudes towards teaching profession of secondary school teachers based on sex, marital status, educational qualification and medium of instruction.
2. To find out the relationship between Professional Ethics of secondary school teachers based on sex, marital status, educational qualification and medium of instruction.
3. To find out whether there is any significant the relationship between Attitude towards teaching profession and professional ethics of secondary school teachers.

Hypotheses

1. There is significant positive relationship between Attitude towards teaching profession of secondary school teachers based on sex, marital status, educational qualification and medium of instruction.
2. There is significant positive relationship between Professional Ethics of secondary school teachers based on sex, marital status, educational qualification and medium of instruction.
3. There is significant positive relationship between Attitude towards teaching profession and professional ethics for secondary school teacher.

Method

Survey method was undertaken for the present study.

Sample

The sample size of the study is Male 27 and Female 63 secondary school teachers. The population for the present study was all those teachers who are teaching all subject at the secondary level in Vellore district (Tamil Nadu). Sampling was done in order get teacher representation 18 secondary schools were randomly drawn from among government, government – aided, private schools.

Tools

V. V. Katti and C.S. Bannur's Attitude towards Teaching Profession Inventory (1974) and the investigator adopted professional ethics tool by A. Punitha Mary. Reliability for professional ethics scale was found to be 0.9333. Internal validity was found to be 0.9660.

Data Analysis

The data were analyzed and interpreted using the statistical techniques correlation analysis and ANOVA.

Table 3.1: Showing the Mean, S.D and t-value for Attitude towards Teaching Profession of Secondary School Teachers based on Sex, Marital Status, Educational Qualification and Medium of Instruction

Variable	Factors		N	Mean	Std. Deviation	t-value	LS
Attitude towards Teaching Profession	Sex	Male	27	164.93	18.096	0.531	NS
		Female	63	166.75	13.344		
	Marital Status	Married	67	166.42	15.277	0.236	NS
		Unmarried	23	165.57	13.816		
	Educational qualification	UG	24	159.71	14.760	2.580	0.01
		PG	66	168.56	14.265		
	Medium of Instruction	Tamil	36	164.97	11.746	2.292	0.05
		English	22	172.77	13.846		

It is inferred from Table 3.1 that UG teachers have been significantly higher than PG teachers in attitude towards teaching profession. English medium teachers have been significantly higher than Tamil medium teachers. It is also inferred from Table 3.1, that there is no significant relationship between secondary school teachers attitude towards teaching profession and sex, marital status.

It is inferred from Table 3.2, that UG teachers have been significantly higher than PG teachers in Professional Ethics. It is also inferred from Table 3.2, that there is no significant difference between secondary teachers Professional Ethics and sex, marital status.

Table 3.2: Showing the Mean, S.D and t-value for Professional Ethics of Secondary School Teachers based on Sex, Marital Status, Educational Qualification and Medium of Instruction

Variable	Factors		N	Mean	Std. Deviation	t-value	LS
Professional Ethics	Sex	Male	27	194.00	16.629	0.844	NS
		Female	63	190.16	20.972		
	Marital Status	Married	67	192.39	19.650	0.882	NS
		Unmarried	23	188.17	20.171		
	Educational qualification	UG	24	178.38	15.670	4.058	0.01
		PG	66	196.02	19.061		
	Medium of Instruction	Tamil	36	187.78	16.385	1.510	NS
		English	22	195.36	21.703		

Table 3.3: Showing the Correlation between Attitude towards Teaching Profession and Professional Ethics of Secondary School Teachers

Variables	N	Mean	Std. Deviation	Attitude towards Teaching Profession	Professional Ethics
Attitude towards Teaching Profession	90	166.20	14.846	1	0.527**
Professional Ethics	90	191.31	19.757	.527**	1

**. Correlation is significant at the 0.01 level

It is evident from Table 3.3, that attitude towards teaching profession and Professional Ethics correlated with each other.

Discussion

The results of this study indicates that secondary school teacher attitude towards teaching profession has been better for UG teachers than PG teachers.

In this project attitude towards teaching profession condition has more contributed for professional ethics. It is related to the result is in line with the findings of Shakuntala K. S and Sabapathy Tara (1999) conducted a study on teacher adjustment as related to interest in and attitude towards teaching. There was a significant and positive correlation between adjustments of secondary school teacher stand their interest in and attitude towards teaching.

Conclusion

Teachers' performance is a crucial input in the field of secondary education. For effective teaching, besides required knowledge and skills, teachers should have favourable attitude towards profession and professional ethics towards teaching profession. A favourable attitude and ethics makes the work not only easier but also more satisfying. Professional ethics is developing attitude conducive to responsible citizenship and to more orderly personal living.

REFERENCES

Devi, N. S. (2005). Assessment of Attitude towards Teaching. Educats, Vol. IV.

Self-learning Material for Teacher Educators, NCERT Campus, New Delhi, Volume II, 2006.

University News, 46(17) April 28-May 04, 2008.

Edu Tracks-June 2008, Vol. 7, No. 10.

Journal of Educational Research Vol. I, No. 1, April-2010.

Edu Tracks, April, 2010 ,Vol. 9, No. 82.

Page 23-29
Recent Trend in Educational Research
Edited by: **Dr. D. Sivakumar**
Edition: **2015**
ISBN: 978-93-5056-741-8
Published by: **Discovery Publishing House Pvt. Ltd., New Delhi (India)**

4

Imbibing Moral Value among Student Teacher's

K. Sheeba[1] and Dr. N. Kalai Arasi[2]

INTRODUCTION

Education is a process of all around development of an individual – physical, intellectual, emotional, social, moral and spiritual. The teacher is expected to function not only as facilitator for acquisition of knowledge but also as inculcator of values and transformer of inner being. As teacher are supposed to look after the total development of children and their performance is the most crucial point in the field of education (POA-1992), training should be adequate to stimulate the socio-cultural, moral development of the child; hence an immediate break through is necessary in teacher education programme. So that it can meet the challenge of value crisis among young generations, which may result in the elapse of the future society. Sockett (1993) argues that techniques of teaching are always sub-servient to a moral end and therefore,

1. Ph.D Scholar, N.K.T. National College of Education for Women, Triplicane, Chennai - 600 005.

2. Associate Professor of Computer Education, N.K.T. National College of Education for Women, Triplicane, Chennai - 600 005.

that the moral character of the teacher is a prime importance. He identifies five major virtues of moral values as follows:

1. *Honesty:* An ability to differentiate between fact and fiction, a concern for the search for truth, an ethic of belief, creation of trust and a passion for truth.
2. *Courage*: A virtue that describes how a person, often selflessly, behaves in difficult and adverse circumstance that demand the use of practical reason and judgment in pursuit of long-term commitments that are morally desirable.
3. *Care:* Teacher care and positive emotions provide the secure base that allows young people to explore and find ways to achieve their own important academic and life goals (Shorey, Synder, Yang and Lewin, 2003).
4. *Fairness*: Teacher assume at lest three roles that involve questions of fairness: distributing time and attention, imposing discipline and sanctions and monitoring fairness as a member of the school.
5. *Practical Wisdom*: Teacher to know what to do when and why, in term of pedagogical skill and content knowledge, with enthusiasm and authencity that the teaching role is congruent with personal values.

Purpose of the Study

This study is a part of a large scale study which is exploring various avenues of student teachers for entering into teaching profession. One of these avenues is how moral value contribute to teaching profession for student teachers. Hence, it is felt necessary to study the changes in the variation in qualification which brings out the difference on the involvement, commitment and dedication to the teaching profession of the student teachers.

Methodology

In this present investigation survey method is adopted. The tool to access the moral value of the student teacher was constructed by the researcher. Sample was collected from 100 D.Ted and 100 B.Ed student teachers, totally 200 samples. Reliability value of the tool is 0.8978 and Validity value of the tool is 0.9475.

Table 4.1: Showing Significance of Difference in Qualification of Student Teacher's among 't' Value of D.Ted, UG with B.Ed. and P.G. With B.Ed in all Selected Variables of Moral Value

	Qualification	N	Mean	Standard Deviation	Std. Error Difference	't' Value	Level of Significance
	1	2	3	4	5	6	7
Honesty	D.Ted	96	46.03	4.459			
	UG with B.Ed	91	45.66	5.184	0.709	0.527	NS
	D.Ted	96	46.03	4.459			
	PG with B.Ed	13	44.46	5.592	1.359	1.155	NS
	UG with B.Ed	91	45.66	5.184			
	PG with B.Ed	13	44.46	5.592	1.552	0.729	NS
Courage	D.Ted	96	33.67	4.509			
	UG with B.Ed	91	33.05	4.571	0.664	0.921	NS
	D.Ted	96	33.67	4.509			
	PG with B.Ed	13	31.00	4.708	1.339	1.991	S 0.05
	UG with B.Ed	91	33.05	4.571			
	PG with B.Ed	13	31.00	4.708	1.360	1.511	S N
Care	D.Ted	96	27.48	3.628			
	UG with B.Ed	91	27.41	3.706	0.536	0.59	NS
	D.Ted	96	27.48	3.628			
	PG with B.Ed	13	24.77	4.549	1.106	2.356	S 0.05
	UG with B.Ed	91	27.41	3.706			
	PG with B.Ed	13	24.77	4.549	1.131	2.332	S 0.05

Contd...

	1	2	3	4	5	6	7
Fairness	D.Ted	96	21.69	2.945			
	UG with B.Ed	91	21.45	2.382	0.391	0.404	NS
	D.Ted	96	21.69	2.945			
	PG with B.Ed	13	19.54	2.295	0.704	2.490	S 0.05
	UG with B.Ed	91	21.45	2.382			
	PG with B.Ed	13	19.54	2.295	0.684	2.796	S 0.01
Practical Wisdom	D.Ted	96	27.58	3.785			
	UG with B.Ed	91	27.44	3.631	0.542	0.265	NS
	D.Ted	96	27.58	3.785			
	PG with B.Ed	13	25.46	3.431	1.027	2.066	S 0.05
	UG with B.Ed	96	27.44	3.631			
	PG with B.Ed	13	25.46	3.431	1.025	1.930	NS
Moral Value Total	D.Ted	96	155.95	16.285			
	UG with B.Ed	91	155.01	16.365	2.389	0.392	NS
	D.Ted	96	155.95	16.285			
	PG with B.Ed	13	145.23	18.722	4.899	2.188	S 0.05
	UG with B.Ed	96	155.01	16.365			
	PG with B.Ed	13	145.23	18.722	4.940	1.980	S 0.05

Objectives

1. To find out whether there is any significant difference between male and female student teachers in their honesty, courage, care, fairness, practical wisdom and moral value - whole.
2. To find out whether there is any significant difference between D.Ted and B.Ed student teacher's in their honesty, courage, care, fairness, practical wisdom and moral value - whole.
3. To find out whether there is any significant difference in qualification of student teachers among D.Ted, UG with B.Ed and PG with B.Ed in their honesty, courage, care, fairness, practical wisdom and moral value - whole.
4. To find out the significant relationship among the student teacher's in their honesty, courage, care, fairness, practical wisdom and moral value - whole.

It is inferred from Table 4.1 that D.Ted qualified student teachers have been significantly better than UG with B.Ed and PG with B.Ed in courage, care, fairness, practical wisdom and moral value as whole.

It is also inferred that there is no significant difference in honesty among D.Ted, UG with B.Ed and PG with B.Ed.

Table 4.2: Showing Significant Relationship among all the Selected Variables of Moral Value

	Honesty	Courage	Care	Fairness	Practical - Wisdom	Moral Value Total
Honesty	1	0.701**	0.682**	0.616**	0.633**	0.882**
Courage	0.701**	1	0.679**	0.576**	0.618**	0.866**
Care	0.682**	0.679**	1	0.651**	0.604**	0.854**
Fairness	0.616**	0.576**	0.651**	1	0.600**	0.783**
Practical Wisdom	0.633**	0.618**	0.604**	0.600**	1	0.814**
Moral Value Total	0.882**	0.866**	0.854**	0.783**	0.814**	1

**. Correlation is significant at the 0.01 level (2-tailed)

It is evident from Table 4.2 that honesty, courage, care, fairness, practical wisdom and moral value total are significantly positively correlated with each other among themselves.

Findings and Discussion

- There is no significant difference between male and female student teachers in their honesty, courage, care, fairness, practical wisdom and moral value as whole.
- There is no significant difference between D.Ted and B.Ed student teachers in their honesty, courage, care, fairness, practical wisdom and moral value as whole.
- D.Ted qualified student teachers have been significantly better than UG with B.Ed and PG with B.Ed in courage, care, fairness, practical wisdom and moral value as whole. This finding is the mirror result of Gott Kim Chaun and Lourdusamy Atputhasamy (2009), in which diploma student teachers faired well than post-graduate student teacher which reveals D.Ted students are very young to enter into the teaching profession when comparated to other groups. Since, they practice the moral values taught by the school immediately in teaching profession they faired well in all prospects of the moral value.
- Their is high positive and significant correlation among the honesty, courage, care, fairness, practical wisdom and moral value as whole. This indicates that future teachers should practice these moral value as whole in an effective manner throughout their teaching profession which will shape them to be successful and remarkable teachers.

Conclusion

Imbibing the moral values like: honesty, courage, care, fairness and practical wisdom becomes the most important goal in the socialization of the student teachers. Children do not expect teacher to be perfect and never make mistakes, but they have little tolerance of hypocrisy, so whatever we ask them, we must be prepared to ask more of ourselves. Hence, effective future student teacher must imbibe to be genuinely honest, courage, care, fairness and practical wisdom to their children/student. It is high time to make the student teachers to realize that there is no greater wisdom than moral value.

REFERENCES

'A Passion for Teaching' – Christopher Day, Routledge Falmen Publication (2004).

'Positive Psychology' – C. R. Synder, Shane J. Lopez, Sage Publication (2007), ISBN: 978-81-7829-924-2-(PB).

'Teacher Education in Singapore' – Goh Kim Chuan and Lourdusamy Atputhasamy (2009).

'Imbibing Values among Students' – Kulwant Singh Pathania, Anuradha D. Pathak, *Edutracks – Journal*, April-2010.

Value Orientation among University B.Ed Students – D. Rajendra Prasad and R. Vijayalatha, Department of Education, Kakatiya University, *Waranpet, Edutrack Journal*, April-2010.

Page 30-36
Recent Trend in Educational Research
Edited by: **Dr. D. Sivakumar**
Edition: **2015**
ISBN: 978-93-5056-741-8
Published by: **Discovery Publishing House Pvt. Ltd., New Delhi (India)**

5

A Study on School Environment and Job Involvement among Middle School Teachers

P. Latha[1] and E. Gomathi[2]

INTRODUCTION

The role of education is the important factor for the development of a nation. It is only education through which the change on a grand scale in the society can be achieved. The teacher has a major role in the educational development. Gandhiji remarked that 'No country can make any progress without good teachers'. The role of the teacher in the educational system is recognized everywhere and at all levels. The teacher is a dynamic force of the school. A school without teacher is just like a body without the soul, a skeleton without flesh and blood, a shadow without substance. There is no greater need for the cause of education today than the need for strong manly men and motherly women as teachers for the young. School Environment here means all those conditions, resources and their integrated and interrelated

1. Ph.D. Research Scholar, N.K.T. National College for Women, Triplicane, Chennai - 600005.
2. Ph.D. Reasearch Scholar, N.K.T. National College for Women, Triplicane, Chennai - 600005.

activities which directly or indirectly affect functioning of the school. A positive correlation is found in such type of performance and school environment. Better is the school environment, better will be the functioning of the school. In an unsuitable environment or opposing environment the possibility of going in opposite direction becomes prominent. The quality of the school-good or bad is reflected by the environment of the school.

Statement of the Problem

"A study on the school environment and job involvement among middle school teachers in Chennai District."

Need and Significance of the Study

Teacher is the 'back bone' of the educational system. National development of a country is directly connected with the quantity and standard of education of its citizens. The quantity and standard of education depends on the quantity and standard of teachers. According to H.G. Wells 'Teacher is the real maker of man'. Teacher is the torch bearer of the race and guardian of the mankind. According to the Humanyunkabir 'Teachers are literally the architects of a nation's destiny'. Teacher is the architect who builds, rebuilds, shapes and reshapes the psychological world of the young member of the society. Education in a controlled environment is essential for human development. School is a special environment where a certain quality of life and certain type of activity and occupation are provided with the job of security, child's development on desirable lines. The conduct of any individual at any time depends in large measure on what objects are in his environment to which he has to respond.

Sample of the Study

Data was collected from the middle school teachers, adopting random sampling method. The total sample sizes 250 were selected for the study belonging to different types of management government, government aided, private schools in Chennai district. For the present investigation the tools used are the school environment questionnaire by Agni kothari. The job involvement inventory by S.P. Sukhia.

Hypotheses – 1

There is no significant relationship between School Environment and Job Involvement among Teachers.

Table 5.1: Correlation between School Environment and Job Involvement among Teachers

Variable	N	'r'-value	Level of Significance
School environment	250	0.730	S*
Job involvement	250		

Note: S* denotes high level of significance.

The calculated value lied between 0.6 to 0.8. Hence there existed highly positive correlation between School Environment and Job Involvement among Teachers. Since the calculated 'r' value was greater than the table value. The null hypothesis is rejected. Thus, There is a significant relationship between school environment and job involvement among teachers.

Hypotheses – 2

There is no significant difference between Male and Female Teachers with respect to their School Environment.

Table 6.2: Showing the Mean and S.D Values of Male and Female Teachers

Variable	Gender	N	Mean	S.D	't' value	Level of Significance
School environment	Male	127	41.5433	7.18658	0.90	NS
	Female	123	42.2358	4.70452		

Note: NS denotes not significant.

Since the calculated 't' value was lesser than the table value. The null hypotheses is accepted. The mean of male teachers is greater than the female teachers .There is no significant difference between male and female teachers with respect to their School Environment.

Hypotheses – 3

There is no significant difference between the U.G and P.G teachers with respect to their School Environment.

Table 5.3: Showing the Mean and S.D Values of U.G and P.G Teachers

Variable	Qualification	N	Mean	S.D	't' value	Level of Significance
School environment	U.G	97	42.3918	4.23664	1.24	NS
	P.G	153	41.5033	7.00388		

Note : NS denotes not significant.

Since the calculated 't' value was lesser than the table value. The null hypotheses is accepted. The mean of U.G qualified teachers is greater than the P.G qualified teachers. There is no significant difference between the U.G and P.G teachers with respect to their School Environment.

Hypotheses – 4

There is no significant difference among Government, Government Aided and Private Teachers with respect to their School Environment.

Table 5.4: 'F'-value of School Environment among Government, Government Aided and Private Teachers

Variable	Degrees of Freedom	Sum of Squares Squares	Mean Sum of	'F'-Ratio	Level of Significance
School environment	2	270.5	135.3	3.73	S*
	247	8955.7	36.3		

Note: S* denotes significant at 0.05 level.

Since the calculated 'F' value was greater than the table value. The null hypothesis is rejected. There is a significant difference among Government, Government Aided and Private Teachers with respect to their School Environment.

Hypotheses – 5

There is no significant difference between male and female teachers with respect to their Job Involvement.

Since the calculated 't' value was lesser than the table value. The null hypotheses is accepted. The mean of male teachers is greater than the female teachers.

Table 5.5: Showing the Mean and S.D Values of the Male and Female Teachers

Variable	Gender	N	Mean	S.D	't' value	Level of Significance
Job involvement	Male	127	117.8583	14.74208	0.50	NS
	Female	123	118.7398	12.79462		

Note: NS denotes not significant.

There is no significant difference between male and female teachers with respect to their Job Involvement.

Hypotheses – 6

There is no significant difference between the U.G and P.G teachers with respect to their Job Involvement.

Table 5.6: Showing the Mean and S.D Values of the U.G and P.G Teachers

Variable	Qualification	N	Mean	S.D	't' value	Level of Significance
Job Involvement	U.G	97	118.2784	11.86885	.075	NS
	P.G	153	118.1503	14.92030		

Note : NS denotes not significant.

Since the calculated 't' value was lesser than the table value. The null hypotheses is accepted. The mean of U.G qualified teachers is greater than the P.G qualified teachers. There is no significant difference between the U.G and P.G teachers with respect to their Job Involvement.

Hypotheses – 7

There is no significant difference among Government, Government Aided and Private Teachers with respect to their Job Involvement.

Since the calculated 'F' value was greater than the table value. The null hypotheses is rejected. There is a significant difference among Government, Government Aided and Private Teachers with respect to their Job Involvement.

Table 5.7: 'F'-value of Job Involvement among Government, Government Aided and Private Teachers

Variable	Degrees of Freedom	Sum of Squares Squares	Mean Sum of	'F'-Ratio	Level of Significance
Job involvement	2	1181	590	3.16	S*
	247	46181	187		

Note: S* denotes significant at 0.05 level.

Discussion

There exists significant relationship between school environment and job involvement. Better school environment made the students to feel pleasure and give their best in their job. While unpleasant environment make the teachers to feel irritable due to lack of facility. Hence this leads to lower their job involvement. This results of the present study is similar with the study which was conducted by Ravikant Chopra (2000). Teachers do not differ in Gender and qualification and their marital status with respect to school environment. But the management wise they statistically differed because private schools have more found which is collected as donations from the students. Hence they maintain good school environment that is why their school environment should be in excellent position to attract the pupil towards the schools.

The poor school environment in the other types of schools due to the scarcity of teachers as such, but due to the scarcity of classrooms. This problem has to be rectified as soon as positive so that the students are given the opportunity to study in a healthy and conducive environment. The male and female teachers do not differ significantly with respect to job involvement. But the Government and Government Aided teachers have more job involvement compared with private teachers. This is due to heavy work load of private teachers as well as they get less salary. So they have more work tension and burden in their profession. Hence they differ in job involvement. The above results are similar with the study conducted by Jesus Livingston (2004).

Conclusion

A few of the teachers face certain problems such as lack of co-ordination and co-operation in the work place. Majority of these teachers are satisfied with their work, job and salary. As expressed by majority of the teachers, they have not got recognition for the job and work done. Majority of the teachers also said that they have promotional opportunities in the teaching profession. A teacher who has a positive job involvement towards his profession can only bring the desirable changes in the child. The teacher should utilize his class as well organized group for attitude development. She/he could try to develop group support for and expression of particular attitudes. Group discussions, seminars, skills drama and other social or group activities may be chosen for developing and organizing group attitude.

The school authorities must ensure good environment for the teacher to have better job involvement and also the higher authorities must allot the work according to the abilities of teacher to avoid heavy work load. The teachers who have good job satisfaction can only make students better citizens of our country.

REFERENCES

Pallwall, M.R. (1985). Teacher Education on the Move: A Global View – Today and Tomarrow. New Delhi.

Khan, M.S. (1983). Teacher Education in India and Abroad. New Delhi. Ashish Publishing House.

Gupta, R.K. (1984). Teacher Education: Current and Prospects. New Delhi. Sterlling.

Rajput, K. Walia (2002). "Teacher Education in India. Sterling Publishers Pvt. Ltd.

Ahmed, S.D (2006), "A Study of Personal and Job Factor as Determinants of Job Involvement for Public Sector High School Teachers in Common Wealth of Pennsylvania", Vol. 45 (5), 1580-A.

Page 37-50
Recent Trend in Educational Research
***Edited by:* Dr. D. Sivakumar**
***Edition:* 2015**
ISBN: 978-93-5056-741-8
***Published by:* Discovery Publishing House Pvt. Ltd., New Delhi (India)**

6

Effect of CAI on Achievement of Disadvantaged Students in Inclusive Setting

Dr. R. Ramar[1] and **Dr. S. S. Jeyabalakrishnan**[2]

INTRODUCTION

Inclusive education means welcoming all children, without discrimination, into regular or ordinary schools. Indeed, it is a focus on creating environments responsive to the differing developmental capacities, needs, and potentials of all children. Inclusion means a shift in services from simply trying to fit the child into 'normal settings'; it is a supplemental support for their disabilities and special needs and promoting the child's overall development in an optimal setting (Evans J. L., 1998). It calls for a respect of difference.

Therefore, the task becomes one of developing the school in response to pupils diversity. This has to include a consideration of overall organization, curriculum and classroom practice, support for learning and staff development (Ainscow, 1997). It does not mean that we should cease to identify and refer to the disabilities of the learners, or to provide particular

1. Vice Principal, PSR College of Education, Sivakasi.
2. Principal, PSR College of Education, Sivakasi.

kinds of support when and where needed. It does mean that we should cease perceiving learners as all being similar because they are referred to by the same name (Bridge and Moss, 1999). The vital factor in inclusive education is that the instruction devised should reach out to all the learners in the classroom, whichever category they may belong to. This is where the computer assisted instruction exactly fits in.

Including Disadvantaged Students in Regular Classrooms

Education in India has historically been the property of the few. Since educational development took place within the framework of a stratified social system; it has always been focused on the needs of the privileged ones. India has made uneven progress in educating its society. The present day Indian society is, therefore, divided into various caste groups and among them the disadvantaged ones continue to remain in the lowest rung of the educational ladder.

After independence, efforts are being made both by the Union Government as well as the State Government to provide numerous facilities to the socially and culturally disadvantaged groups with a view to bring them on par with the various advantaged groups. Tribal people and nomadic people are marginalized sections of our society and they have their own unique culture. They have been cut off from the mainstream for a long time.

The socially and culturally disadvantaged children because of their socio-economic conditions find it hard to be in schools. Quality education is increasingly becoming more expensive over the years. These marginalized groups find it very difficult to afford for such education. They mostly find themselves in residential schools run by the Government specially for them or in such schools that have hostels run by the Government nearby. This group comprises about 15 per cent of the country's total population. Unclean occupations like scavenging, flaying, tanning etc., are most entirely monopolized by these groups. In such a caste based society, access and competencies are invariably possessed by the advantaged groups and so it becomes necessary to take special drive to admit the students from these groups to good schools and to devise some special instructional strategies to enhance the achievement of socially, culturally and academically disadvantaged groups.

Need for the Study

Now-a-days we are passing through the age of information technology wherein knowledge explosion is taking place rapidly in every sphere and new media are being extensively used for transmitting information. Many are unable to keep pace with this phenomenon. This can be attributed to the lack of development of higher mental abilities, self-study habits, initiative on the part of students, etc. The present classroom practice miserably fails to take cognizance of these. Many researchers have made efforts to develop instructional strategies which attempt to take care of the above inadequacies. These researchers have developed instructional strategies comprising various components for teaching a variety of subjects right from school to university. Almost all these researchers have studied the effectiveness of their instructional strategies in terms of achievement and reaction of students towards different components of the strategy as a whole. But, no study has been attempted so far to study the effectiveness of computer assisted instruction with special reference to socially, culturally and academically disadvantaged students.

Computer-assisted instruction (CAI) refers to instruction or remediation presented on a computer. Many educational computer programmes are available online and from computer stores and text-book companies. They enhance teacher instruction in several ways. Computer programmes are interactive and can illustrate a concept through attractive animation, sound, and demonstration. They allow students to progress at their own pace. Computers provide immediate feedback, letting students know whether their answer is correct.

The CAI programmes provide for considerable visualization of objects and processes which are essential for formulation of accurate concepts. What impact a visual presentation can do, any amount of verbal exposition cannot do. Moreover, in a fast developing world, where knowledge explosion is taking place in every sphere, it is unreasonable to expect that the spoken or written words alone could convey the volume of relevant information to the learners. CAI programmes provide unique experience to the learners in the presentation of the content. Computer assisted instruction can penetrate more deeply into human character with an immediate effect and excitement than any other single medium.

Computer assisted instruction caters to individual differences. In the traditional classroom setting, the disadvantaged students are too inhibited to ask the teacher to clarify a concept or to get a doubt cleared. But, in computer assisted instruction, even if they don't understand something at the first attempt, they can understand the concept thoroughly by making use of the provision for playback. Besides, they can also take the software to their houses and listen to or view the instructional programmes according to their own convenience and thereby learn at their own rate without inhibition or the feeling of being preyed upon by the teacher.

Chang *et al.* (2008)/Chai and Tan (2009), Lee and Guo (2009), Daniel (1999), Winter (1994), Stella (1993), Reddy and Ramar (1995, 1999) and Karuppasamy (2011) have studied and established the effectiveness of computer assisted instruction. But no study has been attempted with special reference to disadvantaged students. Systematic researches are, therefore necessary to develop CAI software so as to assess their effectiveness with reference to socially, culturally and academically disadvantaged students.

Objectives

The main objective of the study was to develop CAI software for physics subject of class XI and to assess their effectiveness with special reference to socially, culturally and academically disadvantaged students. Keeping the above main objective in mind the following specific objectives were framed.

1. To find out whether there is any significant difference in the pre-test performance among the control group

students and the students of both the experimental groups. *i.e.,* experimental group I taught through CAI with teacher support system, and experimental group II taught through computer assisted instruction without teacher support systems.

2. To assess whether there is any significant difference in the post-test performance among the control group students and the students of both the experimental groups *i.e.,* experimental group I with teacher support system and the experimental group II without teacher support system.
3. To know whether there is any significant difference in the performance of the control group students and the experimental groups students between pre-test and post-test.
4. To verify whether there exists any significant difference between pre-test and post-test in respect of the various categories of students *i.e.,* socially disadvantaged students, culturally disadvantaged students and academically disadvantaged students in all the groups.
5. To examine whether there is any significant difference in the retention test performance among the control group, the experimental group I with teacher support system and the experimental group II without teacher support system.

Hypotheses

1. There is no significant difference in the pre-test performance among the control group students and the students of both the experimental groups. *i.e.,* experimental group I taught through computer assisted instruction with teacher support system, and experimental group II taught through computer assisted instruction without teacher support systems.
2. There is significant difference in the post-test performance among the control group students and the students of both the experimental groups *i.e.,* experimental group I with teacher support system and the experimental group II without teacher support system.

3. There is significant difference in the performance of the control group students and the experimental groups students between pre-test and post-test.
4. There exists significant difference between pre-test and post-test in respect of the various categories of students *i.e.*, socially disadvantaged students, culturally disadvantaged students and academically disadvantaged students in all the groups.
5. There is significant difference in the retention test performance among the control group. The experimental group I with teacher support system and the experimental group II without teacher support system.

Methodology

Development of CAI Software

An earnest effort was made to develop computer software for CAI. A computer expert was consulted for the purpose and it was discussed with him how to develop software for CAI based on the selected concepts/units. Though there are various CAI programmes such as 'drill and practice programme', 'tutorial programmes', 'generative programme', 'dialogue enquiry programme' and 'simulation programme', the investigator decided to follow the first two *i.e.*, drill and practice and tutorial programmes since these are the most widely used types of computer programmes (Slavin, 1986). Accordingly the CAI software was developed. After validation, it was used in experimental treatment.

Diagrams and sketches were also incorporated in the software in appropriate places through scanning procedure. For subjects and units different codes were allotted. The software was prepared in such a way that it ensured the following.

1. Letting students work at their own pace.
2. Measuring performance quickly and giving students information on their performance.
3. Providing immediate feed back and reinforcement.

Sample

For the purpose of this experiment 75 students from S.S Hindu Nadar Hr. Sec. School, Muhavur were selected. Socially, culturally and academically disadvantaged students were identified on the basis of school records. These students were divided into three groups. Each group consisted of 10 socially disadvantaged students, 5 culturally disadvantaged students and 10 academically disadvantaged students. To see whether the three groups were matched, mean and standard deviation were calculated for their quarterly examination scores. Then F-test was applied. The obtained F-value (0.13) revealed that all the groups were matched ones before the experiment. The control group was taught though traditional lecture method. The experimental group I was taught through CAI with teacher support system and experiment group II was taught through CAI without teacher support system.

Data Collection

A pre-test was conducted to all the groups before the experiment. Then the experiment was conducted for a period of 90 working days. At the end of the experimental period, a post-test was conducted to all the groups. To verify the effect of the applied strategy in terms of retention, a retention test was also conducted to all the groups, after a lapse of 30 days. The responses given by the three groups in pre-test, post-test and retention test formed the vital data required for analysis.

Scoring Procedure

The achievement test consisted of 100 objective type questions. The total score of the test was 100. For each correct answer, the score is one. For each wrong answer the score is zero.

Statistical Techniques Used

The data thus obtained were analysed by using appropriat statistical techniques such as: mean, SD, F-test and t-test.

Findings and Conclusions

1. There is no significant difference in the pre-test performance among the control group students and the students of both the experimental groups. It indicates that all the groups *i.e.*, control group, experimental group I with teacher support system and experimental group II without teacher support system are very much alike in the pre-test performance. All the three groups have shown a matching

and identical performance in pre-test. Therefore, there is no variation between any two groups in terms of achievement in pre-test. Further, the obtained F-value reveals that all the three groups were matched and identical ones before the experimentation. (see Table 6.1)

Table 6.1: Comparison of Pre-test Scores of Control Group and Experimental Groups

Group	N	Mean	S.D	Calculated F-value
Control Group	25	39.2	7.79	0.02 @
Experimental Group I	25	38.6	7.54	
Experimental Group II	25	37.2	7.01	

Note: @ not significant at 0.05 level.

2. There is significant difference in the post-test performance among the control group students and the students of both the experimental groups. The achievement of the students in the experimental groups is higher than the achievement of the students in the control group. The control group students have a mean gain of 0.4. The experimental group I and II have made impressive mean gains amounting to 17.4 and 12.44 respectively. In terms of rate of progress, control group has made a rate of progress amounting to 1.02 per cent which is very insignificant. On the other hand, experimental group I has made a rate of progress amounting to 45.1 per cent and the experimental group II has evinced a rate of progress amounting to 33.44 per cent. In pre-test, the control group and both the experimental groups were matched ones. But in post-test, there is a vast gulf of difference between the control group and experimental groups. Both the experimental groups have evinced vertical progress and impressive rates of progress. The progress as well as the rates of progress made by the experimental groups is the resultant product of the experimental treatment *i.e.*, implementation of computer assisted instruction in the teaching learning process. (see Table 6.2)

Table 6.2: Comparison of Post-test Scores of Control Group and Experimental Groups

Group	N	Mean	S.D	Calculated F-value	Calculated t-value
Control Group	25	39.6	7.69		CG *vs* EGI = 6.67**
Experimental Group I	25	56	9.29	3.39*	CG *vs* EGII = 4.62**
Experimental Group II	25	49.64	7.35		EGI *vs* EGII = 2.63**

Note: *Significant at 0.05 level **Significant at 0.01 level.

3. There is a no significant difference between pre-test and post-test in respect of control group students, whereas there exists significant difference between pre-test and post-test in respect of experimental group I and experimental group II. The control group students could not show any marked progress in achievement in the post-test performance and so there is no significant difference in their performance between pre-test and post-test. On the other hand, the students of both the experimental groups have shown remarkable progress in the post-test achievement. The students of the experimental group I have made a mean gain of 17.4 while the students of the experimental group II have made a mean gain of 12.4. In terms of rate of progress, the students of the experimental group I are far ahead of the students of the experimental group II. The students of experimental group I have shown a rate of progress amounting to 45.1 per cent while the students of the experimental group II have registered 33.4 per cent of rate of progress. In terms of effectiveness, the applied strategy has been effective to both the experimental groups. The difference in the post-test performance between the experimental group I and experimental group II can be attributed to the teacher support system provided to the students of experimental group I Further, this table substantiates the advantage of the applied strategy *i.e.,* computer assisted instruction over the traditional lecture method. (see Table 6.3)

Table 6.3: Comparison of Pre-test and Post-test Scores of Control Group and Experimental Groups

Group	N	Pre-test		Post-test		Calculated t-values
		Mean	S.D	Mean	S.D	
Control Group	25	39.2	7.79	39.6	7.67	0.17 @
Experimental Group I	25	38.6	7.54	56	9.29	7.12**
Experimental Group II	25	37.2	7.01	49.64	7.35	6.00**

Note: @ not significant at 0.05 level **significant at 0.01 level

4. There is significant difference in the performance of students between pre-test and post-test in respect of each category of students in both the experimental groups, whereas there is no significant difference in the performance of the students between pre-test and post-test in respect of each category of students in the control group. Since the control group students were not subjected to the experimental treatment, they could not make any remarkable progress in post-test. On the other hand, all the categories of students in both the experimental groups have done better in the post-test performance than their counterparts in the control group. A comparative study of both the experimental groups brings to light certain interesting revelations. All the categories of students in experimental group I have done better than their respective counterparts in experimental group II. This substantiates the efficacy of the teacher support system provided to the students in experimental group I. This analysis reveals how crucial the role of the teacher is, irrespective of the effectiveness of the strategy applied in the instructional programme. (see Table 6.4)
5. There is significant difference in the retention test performance among the three groups. The students of each of the experimental groups have shown a better performance in the retention test than their counterparts in the control group. This Table 6.5 establishes that the applied strategy *i.e.,* computer assisted instruction has been effective in ensuring retention of the learnt concepts. Here

Table 6.4: Pre-test and Post-test Scores of each Category of Students in all the Groups

Group	Category	N	Pre-test		Post-test		Calculated t-values
			Mean	S.D	Mean	S.D	
Control Group	Socially disadvantaged	10	36	3.58	36.1	3.1	0.06 @
	Culturally disadvantaged	5	30	2.28	31	2.28	0.62 @
	Academically disadvantaged	10	47	4.77	47.4	4.96	0.17 @
Experimental Group I	Socially disadvantaged	10	36	4.24	50.5	4.30	7.20 **
	Culturally disadvantaged	5	29.8	1.72	47	3.03	9.87 **
	Academically disadvantaged	10	46	4.75	66	4.69	8.98 **
Experimental Group II	Socially disadvantaged	10	35	3.22	43.9	3.33	5.76 **
	Culturally disadvantaged	5	28	3.16	45	3.58	7.12 **
	Academically disadvantaged	10	44	3.77	57.7	2.97	8.56 **

Note: @ not significant at 0.05 level ** significant at 0.01 level

also, it is to be noted that the strategy is more effective when it is supplemented with teacher support system. That is why the performance of the students in experimental group I is better than the performance of the students of experimental group II. It can, therefore, be concluded that computer assisted instruction is effective in terms of retention as well as instruction but, when it is complemented with teacher support system, the degree of effectiveness is still higher. (see Table 6.5)

Table 6.5: Comparison of Retention test Scores of all Groups

Group	N	Mean	S.D	Calculated F-value	Calculated t-value
Control Group	25	38.64	7.95		CG *vs* EGI = 5.77**
Experimental Group I	25	53.28	9.54	3.39 *	CG *vs* EGII = 4.09**
Experimental Group II	25	47.52	7.05		EGI *vs* EGII = 2.37**

Note: *significant at 0.05 level **significant at 0.01 level

Implications

1. The results of the study have established that the applied strategy *i.e.,* computer assisted instruction has been more effective than the traditional lecture method in teaching physics to various categories of students at plus one level. Only the degree of efficacy differs from category to category. So similar studies can be attempted in a wide range of schools to arrive at more dependable conclusions.
2. Identifying various categories of students in inclusive classrooms, such as: socially, culturally, and academically disadvantaged students will enable the teachers to devise required remedial instructions to facilitate their learning. The teachers trained in this regard will be able to identify and classify the students into various categories and they will be able to accommodate their instruction to student diversities. Such training can be provided to the teachers at district level by DIET or SSA and at state level by SCERT.
3. CAI and CAL software also can be developed by the NCERT and SCERT and even by commercial agencies since

they are deemed to be more effective to disadvantaged students. So the teachers should be adequately prepared by means of orientation programmes or in-service training to play a supportive role in order to lead the various categories of learners towards optimum level of attainment in inclusive setting.

4. Since the applied mode of instruction enhances the achievement of various disadvantaged students, it will diminish wastage and stagnation in our schools. So the teachers should be adequately prepared by means of orientation programme and such orientation may be given at DIET level also, so that awareness about computer assisted instruction can be developed among the primary school teachers also.

REFERENCES

Ainscow, M. (1997). Towards Inclusive Education. *Times Educational Supplement,* November 1996.

Chai, Ching Sing; Tan, Seng Chee (2009). Professional Development of Teachers for Computer – Supported Collaborative Learning: A Knowledge-building Approach. *Teachers College Record,* Vol. 111, No. 5, pp. 1296-1327.

Chang, Kuo-En; Chen, Yu-Lung; Lin, He-Yan; Sung, Yao-Ting (2008). Effects of Learning Support in Simulation-based Physics Learning. *Computers and Education,* Vol. 51, No. 4, pp. 1486-1498.

Daniel, Joseph I. (1999). Computer-Aided Instruction on the World wide web: The Third Generation. *Journal of Economic Education,* pp. 163-174.

Karuppasamy A. (2011). *Relative Effectiveness of Tutorial and Drill cum Practice Computer Assisted Instructional Programmes on Achievement of Various Categories of Students in Physics.* Ph.D., Thesis. Alagappa University Karaikudi.

Lee, Yu-Fen; Guo, Yuying (2009). Explore Effective use of Computer Simulations for Physics Education *Journal of Computers in Mathematics and Science Teaching,* Vol. 27, No. 4, pp. 443-466.

Ramar, R., Karuppasamy, A. (2011). *Inclusive Education: Challenges and Strategies.* Paper presented in the National Seminar on Inclusive Education at Stella Mary's College of Education, Sivagiri. on 7th and 8th January, 2011.

Ramar, R., Karuppasamy, A. (2011). *Inclusive Education: Theory into Practice*. Paper presented in the National Seminar on Rejuvenating Teacher Education Programmes to Promote Inclusive Schools. held at Jayanthi College of Education on 2nd and 3rd April, 2011.

Ramar, R., Karuppasamy, A. (2011). *Tackling Developmental Disabilities in Inclusive Setting*. Paper presented in the National Seminar on Disability Studies and Inclusive Education: Implications for Policy Perspectives in India Organized by the Social Action and Research foundation, New Delhi.

Reddy, G.L., Ramar, R. (1995a). Effectiveness of Computer Assisted Instruction in Teaching Science to Low Achievers. *Journal of Higher Education,* Vol. 18, No. 2.

Reddy, G.L., and Ramar, R. (1999). Effectiveness of Computer Assisted Instruction in Teaching Science to the Slow Learners. *Research Highlights,* Vol. 12, No. 3.

Stella, (1993). Effectiveness of Computer Assisted Instruction with Special Reference to under – Achievers. *Media and Technology for Human Resource Development,* April 1993. Vol. 5, No. 3.

Winter, Christina Surrency, (1994). A Strategy for Identifying when Interventions should occur in Computer Assisted Instruction. *Dissertation Abstracts International,* Vol. 55, No. 4.

Page 51-58

Recent Trend in Educational Research
Edited by: **Dr. D. Sivakumar**
Edition: **2015**
ISBN: 978-93-5056-741-8
Published by: **Discovery Publishing House Pvt. Ltd., New Delhi (India)**

7

Effect of Personal and Demographic Variables of Teacher Educators of TTIs on their Attitude Towards the Existing Teacher Education Pogramme

R. Shanmugam[1] and Dr. D. Sivakumar[2]

INTRODUCTION

The teacher, a national integrator as he is, is the backbone of society, particularly so in the remote villages. He stands as an outstanding figure among the illiterate and semi-illiterate families. He is their friend, philosopher, and guide. The teacher actively shares the responsibility of reconstructing a social order, with all the cherished values and traditional beliefs, which are being eroded by the surge of new ideals and practices. He acts a social reformer and counsellor to the community.

Indian Education Commission, 1996, (p. 46) states that, "Of all the different factors which influence the quality of education and its contribution to national development, the quality, competence and character of teachers are undoubtedly the most significant. Nothing is more important than securing a sufficient supply of high quality recruits to the teaching

1. Lecturer, Co-operative Teacher Training Institute, Puducherry - 605 001.
2. Associate Professor, Dr. Sivanthi Aditanar College of Education, Tiruchendur.

profession, providing them with the best possible professional preparation and creating satisfactory conditions of work in which they can be fully effective."

The research on teacher education is sparse in Indian context. Moreover, a series of continuous changes crept in organizing the teacher education programmes at different levels in the country. By and large most of the studies focused on aspects like status of elementary school teachers, practice teaching, use of audio-cassette recordings, academic difficulties, micro-teaching, undergraduate training, problems of practicing schools, teaching aptitude, effective school teacher, teacher training as a catalyst of change in professional attitude of student teachers, training of primary teachers in India, relative effectiveness of two models of teacher preparation, professional needs of teacher educators, admission procedures, innovation in teacher training institutions, etc. While most of the studies concentrated around the perception or attitudes of student teachers, some of them were concentrated on the attitudes of teacher educators. It is, therefore, pertinent to collect dada about the attitudes of teacher educators towards the existing teacher education programme so as to get a better picture of the situation and to identify the means to improve the teacher education further which help produce quality teachers. So the present study is an effort in this direction.

Statement of the Problem

The present study investigated as "Effect of Personal and Demographic Variables of Teacher Education of TTIs on their Attitude towards the Existing Teacher Education Programme".

Objectives of the Study

1. To study the attitudes of the teacher educators towards the existing teacher education programme.
2. To identify the differences in the attitudes of the teacher educators depending upon their personal and demographic variable.

Hypotheses

The hypotheses formulated were in 'null-form' as it is akin to statistical testing.

1. The attitude of the teacher educators towards the existing pre-service training programme is not favourable.
2. The personal and demographic variables of the teacher educators do not influence their attitude towards the existing teacher educations progrmme. [This major hypothesis is split into different minor hypothesis for the purpose of testing each variables separately].

Variables Studied

As the present study envisages that the dependent variable is "Attitude of Teacher Educator Towards the Existing Teacher Education Programme" and the independent variables considered in the investigation are teacher educator related personal and demographic variables *viz;* sex, age, educational qualification and experience as primary school teacher.

Methods of the Investigation

The various procedures implemented in the construction and development of data gathering instruments to measure different variables which are included in the study and the methods adapted in selection of sample, collection of data, method of scoring and analysis are as follows.

Construction of Tools

Attitude Scale

For the purpose of developing attitude scale meant for the teacher educators, the investigator consulted the principals, teacher educators, and the related literature and developed items on a five point Likert's type of summated ratings the pilot form of the scale thus finalised was administered on small samples of the teacher educators. Items analysis was carried out to identify the most appropriate items to be included in the final form. The validity and reliability of the scale were also established by using appropriate methods.

Scoring

As the instrument used in this investigation was attitude scale, it was scored by giving the following weightages to the alternative responses. The Likert type attitude scale was scored on a five-point scale by giving weightages 5, 4, 3, 2 and 1 in the case of the positive items and 1, 2, 3, 4 and 5 in the case of negative items respectively. The grand total to each individual on the entire scale was obtained by adding the weightages of all the statements.

Sample

The present investigation is essentially a survey type of research aimed at evaluating the existing pre-service training of the primary school teachers conducted by the 20 TTIs situated in and around of the Puducherry. The investigator considered teacher educators of TTIs was identified by following the cluster sampling technique. Thus, a total of 120 Teacher Educators formed the sample of the survey. Thus, the sampling technique employed in the investigation may be called as two stages stratified random sampling technique.

Collection of the Data

The investigator in person visited all the 20 TTIs and with the permission of the Head of the Institution the Self-Explanatory Instruments developed was administered on 120 Teacher Educators. The Teacher Educators were given the instructions orally and were also asked to read the instructions given along with the instruments and motivated to respond genuinely to all the items in the data gathering tools.

Analysis and Findings

Item-wise analysis was carried out to identify the specific deficiencies in the different aspects of the TTIs. Statistics such as frequencies, percentages and chi-square were employed to make the description more precise. The total scores obtained from all subjects on all variables were completed. Descriptive statistics were used to describe the distribution of the scores. The Inferential statistical technique such as: 't' test and 'F' test were employed to test the different hypotheses.

Description of the Distribution of Teacher Educators' Attitude Scores

The distribution of the attitude scores obtained from the teacher educators are presented in Table 7.1 along with the description statistics such as: mean, median, mode, range, quartile deviation, standard deviation, skewness and kurtosis.

Table 7.1: Showing the Description of the Distribution of Attitudes Score of Teacher Educators

Class Interval	Mid Values	Frequency	Smoothed Frequency	Cumulative Frequencies
70-79	74.5	2	2.33	2
80-89	84.5	5	9.00	7
90-99	94.5	20	16.33	27
100-109	104.5	32	19.21	59
110-119	114.5	26	13.67	85
120-129	124.5	17	14.02	102
130-139	134.5	9	11.00	111
140-149	144.5	72	6.00	118
150-159	154.5	N=120	3.00	120

Mean	:	112.02	Quartile deviation	:	13.172
Median	:	109.29	Standard deviation	:	17.650
Mode	:	103.82	Skewness	:	0.472
Range	:	84.00	Kurtosis	:	0.279

The mean scores obtained by the sample is 112.02 which means the general level of attitude among teacher educators is slightly higher than the average point (35X3=105) on the scale. The values of median and mode 109.29 and 103.82 respectively indicate that the general level of attitude towards the existing teacher education programme among the samples of the subjects is almost at the average level. As the measures of central tendency are in the descending order, the value of mean is more than median, median is also more than mode and the mode is the lowest distribution is said to be positively skewed. Of course it is evident from the calculated value of skewness 0.472. The value of kurtosis 0.279 discloses that the distribution is mesokurtic.

The range of the distributions of scores is 84 (the highest score 154 and the lowest score 70). The quartile deviation and standard deviation are 13.172 and 17.650 respectively. These measures of dispersion reveal that the spread in the distribution is not normal. The relationship between standard deviation and quartile deviation as it exists in the normal probability curve of SD X2/3=Q.D. (*i.e.,* 17.650X2/3=13.172) is not observed in the distribution belongs to the family of normal curves. Thus, the nuli hypotheses that 'the attitude of teacher educators towards the existing pre-service training programme is not favourable, may be accepted.

Table 7.2: Showing the Influence of Sex on Attitude of Teacher Educators

Sl. No.	Variables	Groups	N	M	SD	Df	't' value	Level of Significance at 0.01 Level
1.	Attitudes	Men	52	111.01	17.02	118	1.46	NS
		Women	68	115.96	20.13			

Table 7.2 reveals that the attitude scores obtained by men and women teacher educators reveal that the women teacher educators have scored better than the men teacher educators. The obtained 't' value 1.46 for the difference in the mean scores of men and women teacher educators attitude scores is not statistically significant at the 0.01 level. Hence, the null hypothesis is accepted. It is concluded that there is no significant difference between men and women teacher educators with regard to their attitude towards teacher education programme.

Table 7.3: Showing the Influence of Age on Attitudes of Teacher Educators

Sl. No.	Variables	Groups	N	M	SD	Df	't' value	Level of Significance at 0.01 Level
1.	Attitudes	26-30	82	110.91	19.10	118	0.648	NS
		30 above	38	113.11	16.42			

Table 7.3 reveals that the attitude score of the teacher educators belonging to higher age group have secured a better mean score than their counterparts (113.11>110.91). However, the obtained 't' value of 0.648 is not statistically significant at 0.01 level. Therefore the null hypothesis in accepted. It is concluded that the age of teacher educators does not influence their attitude towards the existing teacher education programme.

Table 7.4: Showing the Influence of Educational Qualification on the Attitude of Teacher Educators

Sl. No.	Variables	Groups	N	M	SD	Df	't' value	Remarks at 0.01 Level
1.	Attitudes	Master degree	77	112.74	18.24	118	1.21	NS
		Master degree above	43	116.64	16.05			

The teacher educators who have better educational qualification have secured better mean score. However the calculated 't' value of 1.21 is found to be statistically not significant at 0.01 level. Hence the null hypothesis that the educational qualification of teacher educators does not significantly influence their attitude is accepted.

Table 7.5: Showing the Influence of Experience as Primary School Teacher on the Attitude of Teacher Educators

Sl. No.	Variables	Groups	N	M	SD	Df	't' value	Level of Significance at 0.01 Level
1.	Attitudes	Without experience as primary school teacher	84	116.57	18.13	118	1.47	NS
		With experience as primary school teacher	36	111.78	15.47			

The obtained 't' value of 1.47 is significant at 0.01 level. Hence the null hypotheses that, the experience as primary school teacher not significantly influence the attitude of teacher educators towards the existing teacher education programme is accepted.

Educational Implications and Recommendations

Thus, the four independent variables namely: age, sex, educational qualification and experience as primary school teacher could not bring any significant difference in the attitude of teacher educators.

It has been identified that the practical aspects of training such as: demonstration lessons, observation lessons, micro-teaching have not been given due importance to develop general and specific skills of teaching in the student teachers.

Most of TTIs shows the library functioning hours is eye-wash, insufficient library books, journals etc., the technical and the non-teaching staff are also insufficient in the TTIs It is often observed that the administrative and academic matters have not been strictly implemented in the TTIs. No doubt our plans are extremely good but their implementation is not satisfactory. Thus producing quality teachers has become a pre requisite to achieve qualitative improvement in education at any level. Self-financing institutions of teacher education is to be stopped, the Government should establish a good number of teacher education institutions in accordance with the man power requirements. All these aspects need immediate attention and suitable remedial action.

Suggestions for further Research

1. The present study is limited to a few personal and demographic variables pertaining to the teacher educators Further researches may also concentrate on other psycho-sociological variables of the subjects involved.
2. Similar study may be undertaken on the TTIs in the Other States.
3. This investigation is limited to a small sample of 120 teacher educators, Future researchers may under take studies with large sample and comparative study.

REFERENCES

Government of India (1989). Guidelines of DIET, Ministry of Human Resource Development, New Delhi.

NCTE (1998). Policy Perspectives in Teacher Education-Critique and Documentation, Government of India, New Delhi.

The National Policy on Education (1986). Programme of Action (1992). Department of Education, Ministry of Human Resource Development, Government of India, New Delhi.

The Report of the Education Commission (1964-66). Education and National Development, Ministry of Human Resource Development, Government of India, New Delhi.

The Report of the National Commission on Teachers-1 (1983-85). Ministry of Education, Government of India, New Delhi.

Page 59-64
Recent Trend in Educational Research
Edited by: **Dr. D. Sivakumar**
Edition: **2015**
ISBN: 978-93-5056-741-8
Published by: **Discovery Publishing House Pvt. Ltd., New Delhi (India)**

8

Metacognitive Awareness of Teachers with Respect to their Selected Demographic Variables

S. Anandaraj[1] and Dr. C. Ramesh[2]

INTRODUCTION

Metacognition is one of the latest buzzwords in educational psychology. It has been over 30 years since the notion of metacognition was introduced into the field of psychology by John Flavell (1979) who is the father of this field. According to him, Metacognition is defined as: '*Knowledge and cognition about cognitive phenomena.*' Metacognition essentially means cognition about cognition. It refers to second order cognitions: thoughts about thought, knowledge about knowledge, or reflections about actions.

Need for the Study

Metacognitive teaching refers teaching with and for metacognition. It means teachers think about their own thinking regarding instructional goals, teaching strategies, sequence, materials, students' characteristics and needs and issues related to curriculum, instruction and assessment before,

1. Research Scholar.
2. Assistant Professor and Head i/c, Department of Education (DD&CE), Manonmaniam Sundaranar University, Tirunelveli.

during and after lessons. Teaching for metacognition means teachers think about how teaching will activate and develop students' metacognition, or thinking about their own thinking as learners. Metacognition enables teachers to regulate their teaching activities according to students, goals and situation. It helps the teachers to plan, monitor and evaluate thinking processes and products, and it also equip the teachers about what information/skills they have, when, why and how to use them. Teachers need to think metacognitively to effectively run teaching and use instructional techniques strategically (Hartman, 2001). So the awareness of metacognition is more important for teachers that why the investigator has under taken this study.

Statement of the Problem

Metacognitive Awareness of Teachers with Respect to Their Selected Demographic Variables.

Definition of the Key Terms

Metacognitive Awareness

It is the awareness of ones's own teaching process and being able to regulate these process to attained the goal.

Teachers

By this, the investigator means those who are working as teacher at the same time they are studying B.Ed degree course in distance education in manonmaniam sundaranar university Tirunelveli.

Demographic Variables

It is the background information about the sample. Here the investigator has selected the gender, major subject and teaching experience of the sample.

Objectives

1. To find out the level of teachers Metacognitive awareness with reference to their Gender, Major subject and Teaching experience.
2. To find whether there is any significant difference between the teachers in their Metacognitive awareness with reference to their Gender, Major subject and Teaching experience.

Null Hypotheses

1. There is no significant difference between the teachers in their Metacognitive awareness with reference to their *(i)* Gender, *(ii)* Major subject, *(iii)* Teaching experience.

Methodology

The researcher used the survey method for the present study. For data collection, the investigator used the standard tool of Metacognitive Awareness Inventory for Teachers (MAIT) prepared by Dr. Cem Balcikanli (2011). The investigator has selected the purposive sample for the present study. It comprises 96 teachers studying B.Ed degree course in distance education in manonmaniam sundaranar university, Tirunelveli. The data were analysed by using Mean, Standard Deviation, 't' test and 'F' test.

Analysis of Data

Table 8.1: Level of Metacognitive Awareness of Teachers with Reference to their Gender, Major Subject and Teaching Experience

Variable	Group	Level of Metacognitive Awareness					
		Low		Average		High	
		No	%	No	%	No	%
Gender	Male	2	16.66	8	66.67	2	16.66
	Female	13	15.48	58	69.04	13	15.48
Major Subject	Arts	10	13.33	54	72.00	11	14.66
	Science	4	19.05	12	57.14	5	23.81
Teaching Experience (in years)	2-7	4	12.50	22	68.8	6	18.7
	8-13	3	14.29	14	66.66	4	19.05
	14-19	5	20.83	14	58.33	5	20.83
	20-25	2	10.52	15	78.95	2	10.52

Table 8.1 reveals that, 16.66 per cent of male teachers have low, 66.67 per cent of them have moderate and 16.66 per cent of them have high level of metacognitive awareness. 15.48 per cent of female teachers have low, 69.04 per cent of them have moderate and 15.48 per cent of them have high level of metacognitive awareness. 13.33 per cent of arts teachers have low, 72 per cent of them have moderate and 14.66 per cent of

them have high level of metacognitive awareness. 19.05 per cent of science teachers have low, 57.14 per cent of them have moderate and 23.81 per cent of them have high level of metacognitive awareness. 12.50 per cent of 2-7 years teaching experience teachers have low, 68.8 per cent of them have moderate and 18.7 per cent of them have high level of metacognitive awareness. 14.29 per cent of 8-13 years teaching experience teachers have low, 66.66 per cent of them have moderate and 19.05 per cent of them have high level of metacognitive awareness. 20.83 per cent of 14-19 years teaching experience teachers have low, 58.33 per cent of them have moderate and 20.83 per cent of them have high level of metacognitive awareness. 10.52 per cent of 20-25 years teaching experience teachers have low, 78.95 per cent of them have moderate and 10.52 per cent of them have high level of metacognitive awareness.

Table 8.2: Difference between the Teachers in their Metacognitive Awareness with Reference to their Gender and Major Subject

Variable		N	Mean	SD	Calculated 't' value	Remarks at 5% Level
Gender	Male	12	103.83	7.322	1.547	NS
	Female	84	100.23	9.015		
Major Subject	Arts	75	100.12	7.975	0.951	NS
	Science	21	102.67	11.53		

(for df 94 at 5% level of significance, the table value of 't' is 1.98)

Table 8.2 reveals that there is no significant difference between the teachers in their metacognitive awareness with reference to their gender and major subject.

Table 8.3: Deference among the Teachers in their Metacognitive Awareness with Reference to their Teaching Experience

Variable	Source of Variance	Sum of Square	Mean Square	df	'F' value	Table value	Remarks (5% level of significance)
Teaching Experience	Between	576.51	192.17	3	2.56	2.71	NS
	Within	6894.47	74.94	92			

Table 8.3 reveals that there is no significant difference among the teachers in their metacognitive awareness with reference to their teaching experience. Hence the null hypothesis is accepted.

Findings and Interpretation

The major conclusions derived from the study are:

1. The level of teachers in their metacognitive awareness is found to be average in terms of their gender, major subject and teaching experience.
2. There is no significant difference between the teachers in their metacognitive awareness with reference to their gender and major subject.
3. There is no significant difference among the teachers in their metacognitive awareness with reference to their teaching experience.

Suggestions

- Teachers should improve their teaching skills to compensate the weakness of their teaching style.
- Before taking the class the teachers should have the planned knowledge about what are the teaching aids I have to be use.
- Teachers should regulate themselves while teaching to attain the objectives.
- After completing the class the teachers should check whether I have reached the goal or not.
- The teacher educator should create the awareness of their knowledge and how to regulate it effectively in teaching learning process.

REFERENCES

Best, J. W. and Khan J.V., *Research in Education.* New Delhi: Prentice Hall of India Private Limited, (2006).

http://www.investigacion-psicopedagogica.org/revista/articulos/25/english/Art_25_563.pdf accessed on 20-12-2012.

http://www.c-s-p.org/flyers/9781847185785-sample.pdf accessed on 28-12-2012.

http://www.lifecircles-inc.com/Learningtheories/constructivism/flavell.html accessed on 28-12-2012.

http://www.shodhganga.inflibnet.ac.in accessed on 28-12-2012.

http://www.academia.edu/501886/do_metacognitively_aware_teachers_make_any_difference_in_studentsmetacogniton accessed on 28-12-2012.

Page 65-71
Recent Trend in Educational Research
***Edited by:* Dr. D. Sivakumar**
***Edition:* 2015**
ISBN: 978-93-5056-741-8
***Published by:* Discovery Publishing House Pvt. Ltd., New Delhi (India)**

9

Awareness of Dengue Fever among Secondary School Students in Pudukkottai District

Chandrasekar S and Arunkumar J

INTRODUCTION

Dengue fever is an infected disease carried by mosquitoes by any four related dengue virus DEN-1, DEN-2, DEN-3 and DEN-4. This disease used to be called 'break bone' fever because it sometimes causes severe joint and muscle pain that feels are bones are breaking, hence the name. Dengue fever is found mostly during and shortly after the rainy season tropical and sub-tropical areas of Africa, Southeast Asia, China, India and South America. Two main species of the mosquito Aedes aegypti and Aedes albopictus have been responsible for all cases of dengue transmitted in this country. Dengue is not contagious from person to person. Symptoms include high fever up to 105F, headache, severe joint, muscle pain, nausea, vomiting and swollen lymph nodes. A test that may be done to diagnose this condition include Antibody titer for dengue virus types, Complete blood count (CBC) and Polymerase chain reaction (PCR) test for dengue virus types.

Assistant Professors, Sudharsan College of Education, Perumanadu, Pudukkottai.

There is no specific treatment for dengue fever. You will need fluids it there are signs of dehydration. Acetaminophen is used to treat a high fever. The best way to prevent dengue virus infection is to take special precautions to avoid being bitten by mosquitoes. Several dengue vaccines are being developed, but none is likely to be licensed by the food and drug administration in the next few years.

The present study is aimed at identifying the awareness of dengue fever among secondary school students aims at offering meaningful suggestions for improving the awareness of dengue fever among the secondary school students.

Statement of the Problem

The present study is concerned with the awareness of dengue fever in secondary school students in Pudukkottai district. It examines the difference on the awareness of boys and girls, rural and urban students and the nature of the school.

Objectives

The following are the main objectives of the present study.

1. To study the awareness of dengue fever in secondary school students in Pudukkottai district with reference to boys and girls.
2. To study the awareness of dengue fever in secondary school students in Pudukkottai district with reference to rural and urban school students.
3. To study the awareness of dengue fever in secondary school students in Pudukkottai district with reference to co-education and girls school students.
4. To study the awareness of dengue fever in secondary school students in Pudukkottai district with reference to co-education and boys school students.
5. To study the awareness of dengue fever in secondary school students in Pudukkottai district with reference to boys and girls school students.

Hypotheses

To realize the above objectives the following hypotheses in the null form are formulated for testing.

1. There would be no significant difference between boys and girls in their awareness of dengue fever in secondary school students.
2. There would be no significant difference between rural and urban school students in their awareness of dengue fever in secondary school students.
3. There would be no significant difference between co-education and girls school students in their awareness of dengue fever in secondary school students.
4. There would be no significant difference between co-education and boys school students in their awareness of dengue fever in secondary school students.
5. There would be no significant difference between the boys school and girls school students in their awareness of dengue fever in secondary school students.

Methodology

In the present study normative survey method of investigation was employed. A sample of 296 secondary school students was selected from Pudukkottai district. The investigator himself developed a questionnaire for identifying awareness of dengue fever among secondary school students. The tool contains 25 items. Each item two responses are given 'YES'/'NO' alternatives. For 'YES' one (1) Mark is given and for 'NO' zero (0) mark. The range of scores is 0 to 25. The following statistical technique were used Mean, S.D, and 't' test was employed.

Analysis and Interpretation of the Data

Hypothesis – 1

There would be no significant difference between boys and girls in their awareness of dengue fever in secondary school students.

Table 9.1: Showing Mean, SD and t-value of Boys and Girls Secondary School Students with Awareness of Dengue Fever

Variable	No	Mean	SD	Calculated 't' value	Remark at 5% Level
Boys	138	83.68	10.63	0.5	Not significant
Girls	158	83.39	8.72		

The calculated 't' value 0.5 at the 5 per cent level is less than the table value 1.96 with 294 degrees of freedom. Hence the null hypothesis is accepted. It is concluded that there is no significant difference in the awareness of dengue fever in boys and girls among secondary school students.

Hypothesis – 2

There would be no significant difference between rural and urban in their awareness of dengue fever in secondary school students.

Table 9.2: Showing Mean, SD and t-value of Rural and Urban Secondary School Students with Awareness of Dengue Fever

Variable	No	Mean	SD	Calculated 't' value	Remark at 5% Level
Rural	186	84.19	9.52	1.56	Not significant
Urban	110	82.6	8		

The calculated 't' value 1.56 at the 5 per cent level is less than the table value 1.96 with 294 degrees of freedom. Hence the null hypothesis is accepted. It is concluded that there is no significant difference in the awareness of dengue fever in rural and urban among secondary school students.

Hypotheses – 3

There would be no significant difference between co-education and girls school students in their awareness of dengue fever in secondary school students.

Table 9.3: Showing Mean, SD and t-value of Co-education and Girls School Secondary Students with Awareness of Dengue Fever

Variable	No	Mean	SD	Calculated 't' value	Remark at 5% Level
Co-education school	120	82.96	9.6	0.74	Not significant
Girls school	100	83.86	8.48		

The calculated 't' value 0.74 at the 5 per cent level is less than the table value 1.96 with 218 degrees of freedom. Hence the null hypothesis is accepted. It is concluded that there is no significant difference in the awareness of dengue fever in co-education and girls' school among secondary school students.

Hypotheses – 4

There would be no significant difference between co-education and boys school students in their awareness of dengue fever in secondary school students.

Table 9.4: Showing Mean, SD and t-value of Co-education and Boys School Secondary Students with Awareness of Dengue Fever

Variable	No	Mean	SD	Calculated 't' value	Remark at 5% Level
Co-education school	120	82.96	9.6	0.65	Not significant
Boys school	76	83.97	11.2		

The calculated 't' value 0.65 at the 5 per cent level is less than the table value 1.96 with 194 degrees of freedom. Hence the null hypothesis is accepted. It is concluded that there is no significant difference in the awareness of dengue fever in co-education and boys school among secondary school students.

Hypotheses – 5

There would be no significant difference between boy's school and girls school students in their awareness of dengue fever in secondary school students.

Table 9.5: Showing Mean, SD and t-value of Boy's School and Girls School Secondary Students with Awareness of Dengue Fever

Variable	No	Mean	SD	Calculated 't' value	Remark at 5% Level
Boys school	76	83.97	11.2	0.07	Not significant
Girls school	100	83.86	8.48		

The calculated 't' value 0.07 at the 5 per cent level is less than the table value 1.96 with 174 degrees of freedom. Hence the null hypothesis is accepted. It is concluded that there is no significant difference in the awareness of dengue fever in boys' and girls' school among secondary school students.

Major Findings of the Study

1. There is no significant difference between boys and girls in their awareness of dengue fever in secondary school students.
2. There is no significant difference between rural and urban school students in their awareness of dengue fever in secondary school students.
3. There is no significant difference between co-education and girls school students in their awareness of dengue fever in secondary school students.
4. There is no significant difference between co-education and boys school students in their awareness of dengue fever in secondary school students.
5. There is no significant difference between the boys school and girls school students in their awareness of dengue fever in secondary school students.

Recommendations

The investigator makes the following suggestions in order to disseminate information and knowledge awareness of dengue fever among secondary school students.

- Government may take necessary steps to give more exposure in dengue fever via mass media.
- Schools can be conducted seminar, group discussion, debates and essay competition on vector borne diseases.
- Co-curricular and extracurricular activities should be encouraged to promote awareness on vector borne diseases.
- Periodical meetings can be conducted by inviting experts in the field of vector borne diseases.

Conclusion

The research studies on the awareness of dengue fever among secondary school students – Gender, locality of schools, the nature of the school are carried by researchers. There is no significant difference in the mean scores of aware of dengue fever among school students in relation to gender, locality and nature of the school.

REFERENCES

Amul B. Patel and Hitesh Rathod. *et al.* (2011). Perceptions Regarding Mosquito Borne Diseases in an Urban area of Rajkot City, *National Journal of Medical Research,* Vol. 1 Issue 2 Oct-Dec. 2011, pp. 45-47 ISSN 2249 4995.

Boratne A.V and V. Jayanthi. *et al.* (2010). *Predictors of Knowledge of Selected Mosquito-borne Diseases among Adults of Selected Peri-urban Areas of Puducherry,* J Vector Borne Dis 47, December 2010, pp. 249-256.

Kothari C. R, (2012). Research Methodology: Methods and Techniques, New Age International Publishers, New Delhi.

Best and Kahn, (2006). Research in Education, PHI Learning Private Limited, New Delhi.

www.wikipedia.com

http://www.cdc.gov/dengue/

http://www.thehindu.com/todays-paper/tp-national/tp-tamilnadu/stress-on-proper-test-for-dengue/article4281961.ece

http://newindianexpress.com/cities/bangalore/article575845.ece

http://newindianexpress.com/lifestyle/health/article202162.ece

Page 72-79

Recent Trend in Educational Research
Edited by: **Dr. D. Sivakumar**
Edition: **2015**
ISBN: 978-93-5056-741-8
Published by: **Discovery Publishing House Pvt. Ltd., New Delhi (India)**

10

A Study on AIDS Awareness and Attitude of Prospective Teachers Towards AIDS

P. Latha[1] and T. Dhanalakshmi[2]

INTRODUCTION

The 2011 UNAIDS report highlights that there are early signs that HIV treatment is having a significant impact on reducing the number of new HIV infections. According to UNAIDS estimates, there are now 34 million people living with HIV. During 2010 some 2.7 million people became newly infected with the virus, including an estimated 390,000 children and 1.8 million people death from AIDS. The most tragic aspect is that about half of the infected victims are in the most productive age group of 15-24 years.

As compared to the rest of the world AIDS is spreading rapidly in India. As per the HIV estimations 2010, India is estimated to have 23.9 lakhs people infected with HIV, at an estimated adult HIV prevalence of 0.31 per cent, Adult HIV prevalence among men is 0.36 per cent, while among women, it is 0.25 per cent.

1. Associate Professor of Physical Science.
2. Annammal College of Education for Women, Thoothukudi - 628 003.

The WHO SEARO office contracted Alliance's Regional Technical Support Hub to undertake a situation analysis of HIV/AIDS among transgender populations and the national responses for them in nine South and South-East Asian Counties. This review highlights the need for improved advocacy efforts and a greater national response to save the lives of these populations who are at risk for HIV infection.

According to Florence David (1982) "A compelling argument for introducing structured sex education in classrooms is the crying need to provide accurate information on sex and sexuality by trained teachers, counselors and parents. The level of awareness among adolescent Indian children on matters of sexuality is rock-bottom where neither parents nor teachers offer advice and information. Moreover the rapid spread of HIV/AIDS in India necessitates sex education, so that young people can take safe and responsible sex-related decisions."

The world's second most populous country, India, is experiencing a highly varied HIV epidemic, which appears to be stable or diminishing in some parts while growing at a modest rate in others. If the same alarmingly increasing trend of HIV infection continues, India will not only have the largest number of AIDS cases in the world but will also account of 40 per cent of global estimates as per Harvard AIDS institute's projections. Since there is no effective cure or vaccine for the disease, awareness remains the only safeguard for its prevention.

Need for the Present Study

The expansion and improvement of HIV and AIDS education around the world is critical to preventing the spread of HIV. Therefore, currently the major thrust is on information, education and communication (IEC) campaign to make people aware in order to prevent further spread of HIV infection. According to the WHO more than half world's HIV/AIDS population below the age of 25 (80%) live in developing countries. These young people are both an important target group and a potential resource for the prevention of HIV and STD infection.

Students are considered at greater risk of contracting HIV infection due to lack of knowledge and their tendency of experimenting high risk behaviours, especially unsafe sexual practices and intravenous drugs use as a result of curiosity and relatively more freedom in the college. (Lawrence *et al*. 1990 and Benara *et al*. 1992). Studies have been carried out among different levels of students and professional college students throughout India (Chandra *et al*. 1993, Panna Lal *et al*. 1994).

This study was taken up to know the awareness and attitude of prospective teachers towards AIDS in the Thoothukudi district only. Teaching profession demands a clear set of goals, love for profession, good interpersonal and intrapersonal skills and obviously a favorable attitude towards the profession. As student-teachers, they will be required not only to acquire proficiency in planning of the lessons and delivery but also must have good knowledge and good attitude towards the entire field.

Teachers are the main responsible people for creating a good society. If they are having awareness in the entire field, it will reach the many generations of the students easily. They are the tool to carrying out the messages into the entire society. So the investigator conducted her study on prospective teachers.

The present study undertaken is important in today's Indian context. It will throw light on the significance areas of AIDS awareness and attitude towards AIDS in a broad perspective. It would add to the knowledge of academic institutions, public and social institutions.

Objectives

1. To study the significant difference between the sub-samples of prospective teachers with respect to AIDS awareness and their attitude towards AIDS.
2. To find out the significant relationship between AIDS Awareness and Attitude of prospective teachers towards AIDS.

Null Hypotheses

1. There is no significant difference in AIDS awareness between: male and female prospective teachers; prospective teachers from rural and urban colleges; graduate and post graduate prospective teachers; arts and science prospective teachers; government aided and private college prospective teachers.
2. There is no significant difference in the attitude of prospective teachers towards AIDS between the five sub-samples of prospective teachers as in hypothesis (1).

Method

The Survey method was used for studying the problem.

Sample

The sample consisting of 250 prospective teachers from Thoothukudi educational district was selected using stratified random sampling techniques.

Tools

The AIDS awareness questionnaire developed by D.S. Prasad (2007) was used to measure AIDS awareness. It consisted of 37 questions. The scoring key consisted of four alternatives among which, one is the correct answer.

Attitude towards AIDS inventory was constructed and validated by the investigators (2012). This inventory consisted of 27 items, in the form of both positive and negative statements. Each statement was set against a five point scale of 'strongly agree', 'agree', 'undecided', 'disagree' and 'strongly disagree'. The scores ranged from 27 to 135. The reliability of the inventory was found to be very high with a value of 0.99.

Table 10.1 , the 't' test with respect to AIDS awareness at 0.05 level of significance shows that there is a significant difference between Prospective teachers from urban and rural areas and from Government Aided and Private Management colleges. But there is no significant difference between males and females, between under graduate and post-graduate prospective teachers and between Arts and Science Major prospective teachers.

Analysis of Results

Table 10.1: Test of Significant Difference in AIDS Awareness of Prospective Teachers with Respect to Sub-samples

Variables	Category	N	Mean	S.D.	Calculated 't' value	Remarks at 5% Level
Gender	Male	73	19.34	4.715	1.070	NS
	Female	177	20.01	3.909		
Type of Locality	Rural	104	18.95	4.257	2.779	S
	Urban	146	20.43	3.995		
Qualification	U.G	157	19.75	4.235	0.353	NS
	P.G.	93	19.94	4.056		
Major	Arts	105	19.81	4.335	0.021	NS
	Science	145	19.82	4.048		
Management	Government Aided	103	21.05	3.666	4.149	S
	Private	147	18.96	4.282		

Table 10.2: Test of Significant Difference in the Attitude of Prospective Teachers towards AIDS with Eespect to Sub-samples

Variables	Category	N	Mean	S.D	Calculated 't' value	Remarks at 5% Level
Gender	Male	73	98.45	15.987	1.989	S
	Female	177	102.81	15.138		
Type of Locality	Rural	104	100.37	15.077	1.016	NS
	Urban	146	102.37	15.769		
Qualification	U.G	157	100.80	15.047	0.955	NS
	P.G.	93	102.77	16.207		
Major	Arts	105	98.47	15.713	2.680	S
	Science	45	103.76	14.984		
Management	Government Aided	103	103.22	14.942	1.460	NS
	Private	147	100.35	15.798		

Table 10.2, the 't' test with respect to attitude of prospective teachers towards AIDS at 0.05 level of significance shows that there is a significant difference between males and females and between Arts and Science Major prospective teachers. But there is no significant difference between Prospective teachers from

urban and rural areas, between under graduate and post-graduate prospective teachers and from Government aided and Private Management colleges.

Findings

- Both male and female prospective teachers have equal level of AIDS awareness.
- The AIDS awareness of the urban prospective teachers is found to be more than the rural students.
- Both U.G and P.G. students have equal level of AIDS awareness.
- Prospective teachers belonging to Arts and Science Major have equal level of AIDS awareness with respect to major.
- The AIDS awareness of government aided college students is found to be more than the private college students.
- Female prospective teachers have positive attitude towards AIDS than male prospective teachers.
- Both rural and urban prospective teachers have the same attitude towards AIDS.
- Both U.G. and P.G. prospective teachers have the same attitude towards AIDS.
- Science major prospective teachers have positive attitude towards AIDS than arts major prospective teachers.
- Both government and private college prospective teachers have the same attitude towards AIDS.

Interpretation

Rural area college students do not have more AIDS awareness, because they are not exposed to many awareness programmes. Rural area people feel shy to talk about sex related issues. They are also brought up that it is wrong.

Many orientation programmes are conducted for government aided college students regarding AIDS. But private colleges are not much interested in conducting social welfare programmes. So the students are unaware of AIDS. Moreover most of the government aided college students belong to higher social strata. They have wide exposure to mass media and technology which give them awareness.

In our society educational attainment of female students are high compared to male students. Mass media like T.V., cinema are widely viewed by female than male. Hence they contribute largely towards AIDS awareness. So their attitude towards AIDS is positive.

Science major students have high level of attitude towards AIDS compared to arts major students. The science students gain more knowledge about various diseases through their subject. So they have high level of awareness.

Conclusion

The utilization of mass media as a channel for communication and dissemination of HIV/AIDS information has been a very effective tool for HIV/AIDS awareness campaigns in recent years. The progress made in programmes designed to raise this understanding has been quite remarkable, and mass media remains the most practical means of conveyance of accurate knowledge about HIV/AIDS, if given the high level of public accessibility to various forms of media, particularly television and internet. Employing mass media as the primary resource for the propagation of the HIV/AIDS youth awareness campaign, has proved to be of inestimable value, in raising public awareness. Red Ribbon Club is a movement started by the Government of India in Schools through which students will be having awareness about AIDS. Red Ribbon Club Programme (RRCP) is a comprehensive, promotional and preventive intervention to enhance voluntary blood donation as well as mainstream HIV and AIDS prevention.

The results therefore suggest the need for AIDS awareness to be given for the younger students. The government and non-governmental agencies and volunteers should give AIDS awareness to all people particularly female students, young people and those who belong to rural areas. The AIDS awareness should prevent them from AIDS in future, because nowadays children and adolescent people are more affected by HIV/AIDS. Moreover the increasing level of AIDS awareness will create positive attitude towards HIV/AIDS.

REFERENCES

AIDS, (1995). Tamil Nadu AIDS Control Society, Chennai, Print Deal.

AIDS, (1996). Emma Trust Society Publisher, Chennai.

Henderson, Tina Burlean (2004). "An Attributional Analysis of African Clergy's Attitudes on HIV/AIDS", *Dissertation Abstracts International* Vol. 66, No. 3, p. 1005 - Sep 2005.

Kalra. R.M, Kalra. S, (1998). *"Adolescents of AIDS"*, Delhi, Vikas Publishing House Pvt. Ltd.

Kniss, Darrel Dean (2007). "Sexuality and HIV Education, Knowledge, Attitudes and Behaviours of Young Adults", *Dissertation Abstracts International* Vol. 68, No. 3, - Sep 2007.

Mannangatty. S, Zayapragassarazan. Z and Minnel Kodi. B (2008). "Awareness, Knowledge, Attitude and Beliefs Regarding HIV/ AIDS among the Engineering College Students of Puducherry", *Edutracks* Vol. 7, No. 11, p. 37 - July 2008.

Parul Chopra, Rageshree Niyogi, (2010). *Adolescence the Wonder Years*, Delhi, Word Books Pvt. Ltd.

Ranjitha S Shetty, Sanjay Pattanshetty, Asha Kamath, Sneha Kamath (2010). "Awareness of HIV/AIDS in Eural India", *Australian Medical Journal* Vol. 3, No. 10-2010.

Tung, WC Ding, K Farmer, S AF Tung, Wei-Chen Ding, Kele (2008). "Knowledge, Attitudes, and Behaviours Related to HIV and AIDS among College Students in Taiwan", *Janac Journal of the Association of Nurses in AIDS care*, Vol. 19, No. 5, p. 397 – Sep. 2008.

Page 80-85
Recent Trend in Educational Research
***Edited by:* Dr. D. Sivakumar**
***Edition:* 2015**
ISBN: 978-93-5056-741-8
***Published by:* Discovery Publishing House Pvt. Ltd., New Delhi (India)**

11

Attitude towards 3G Technologies among Student – Teachers in Colleges of Education

Dr. G. Manimaran[1], G. Anitha[2] and S. Sangeetha[2]

INTRODUCTION

Mobile tele-communication system continuously progresses with the advancement of technology and the users' demands towards transmission speed and application services. The acceleration of the demand for high speed data services and the spreading of mobile communication have also increased the demand for high speed mobile services. Parallel to these tendencies, studies for investing and developing new technologies in communication have been initiated. Mobile services and 3G technologies have become a fundamental part of people's lives throughout the world. There has been a steady growth in worldwide 3G mobile adoption. Mobile internet adoption is expected to exhibit a fast growth in the following years, achieving up to 40 per cent of total subscribers in 2013. However, there also exists a wide range of 3G diffusion levels in countries.

1. Principal, Indra Ganesan College of Education, Tiruchirappalli.
2. Asst. Professors, Indra Ganesan College of Education, Tiruchirappalli.

Need for the Study

Education is a life long process therefore anytime anywhere access to it is the need. Information explosion is an ever increasing phenomena. Therefore there is necessary to get access to this information. Education should meet the needs of variety of learners and therefore IT is important in meeting this need. Since the Education is going to be transmitting to the society through Student - Teachers, who are the future Teachers, they should posses Technological literacy. Investigators are very much interested to find the level of Technological Literacy such as 3G Technology among Student - Teachers; they coined the topic as: "Attitude towards 3G Technologies among Student - Teachers in Colleges of Education".

Objectives of the Study

The objectives of the study are: *(i)* To measure the level of Attitude towards 3G Technology among Student - Teachers in Colleges of Education. *(ii)* To measure the level of significant difference on the Attitude towards 3G Technology among Male and Female, Arts and Science Student - Teachers and Student - Teachers who are having own Computer and not having own Computer and Student - Teachers who are using Internet Weekly and who are using Internet Monthly.

Hypotheses

The Null hypotheses were formulated to realize the above objectives.

Nature of the Research

As the study aimed to measure the Attitude towards 3G Technology among Student - Teachers in Colleges of Education, it is a Normative Survey Research.

Development of Tool

Attitude towards 3G Technology Scale (AT3GTS) standardized by Suresh Kumar and Karthikeyan (2011) has been used by the investigators to measure the Attitude towards 3G Technology. It is a five point Scale consists of 30 items.

Sample Selection

Investigators used Systematic Random Sampling Technique and selected Student - Teachers from 3 Self-Finance Colleges of

Education in Tiruchirappalli District as samples. The AT3GTS were given to the 104 Student - Teachers. The filled – in questionnaires were received from them were 98. The total samples have been classified further on the basis of Gender, Subject, Computer ownership and frequency of Utilization Internet.

Table 11.1: Sample Distribution

Sl. No.	Category	Size	Percentage
1.	Male	26	27
	Female	72	73
2.	Arts	40	41
	Science	58	59
3.	Having own Computer	45	46
	Not having own Computer	53	54
4.	Using Internet Weekly	30	31
	Using Internet Monthly	68	69

Data Analysis

Thus the data collected in this manner undertake analysis by using different statistical technique. Mean and SD were calculated for each Variables to calculate 't' values which is the test of significance of the difference between two Means.

Table 11.2: Mean and SD of the Student - Teachers towards Awareness on 3G Technology among Student - Teachers with Different Category

Sl. No.	Components		N	Mean	SD
1.	Total		98	61.8	10.0
2.	Gender	Male	26	61.72	9.76
		Female	72	61.87	10.10
3.	Subject	Arts	40	60.47	10.9
		Science	58	62.77	19.21
4.	Computer Ownership	Own Computer	45	62.99	8.69
		Not own Computer	53	60.84	10.90
5.	Frequency of Utilization Internet	Weekly	30	63.09	8.20
		Monthly	68	61.28	10.70

From Table 11.2 it is revealed that the average Mean Score of the Attitude towards 3G Technology Score is 61.8 Moreover the minimum score is 60.47 and the maximum score is 63.09. This reveals Attitude towards 3G Technology was good among Student - Teachers.

Table 11.3: Significance Difference on the Mean Scores of Male and Female Student - Teachers towards Awareness on 3G Technology

Category	N	Mean	SD	t-value	Remarks
Male	26	61.72	9.76	0.066	NS
Female	72	61.87	10.1		

NS: Not Significant
S: Significant

From Table 11.3 it is understood that the 't' value 0.066 shows that there is no significant difference at 0.05 level. On observing the Mean Scores among Male and Female Student - Teachers with respect to the Attitude towards 3G Technology are similar. Hence the framed Null Hypothesis is accepted.

Table 11.4: Significance Difference on the Mean Scores of Arts and Science Student - Teachers towards Awareness on 3G Technology

Category	N	Mean	SD	t-value	Remarks
Arts	40	60.47	10.91	1.092	NS
Science	58	62.77	9.2		

NS: Not Significant
S: Significant

The 't' value 1.092 from Table 11.4 shows that it is not significant at 0.05 level. The result shows that the Mean Scores among Arts and Science Student - Teachers with respect to the Attitude towards 3G Technology are similar. Hence the framed Null Hypothesis is accepted.

From Table 11.5 it is seen that the 't' value 1.085 is not significant at 0.05 level. These results show that the Mean Scores of Student - Teachers who were having own Computer and not having own Computer with respect to the Attitude towards 3G Technology are similar. Hence the framed Null Hypothesis is accepted.

Table 11.5: Significance Difference on the Mean Scores of Student - Teachers who were having own Computer and not having own Computer towards Awareness on 3G Technology

Category	N	Mean	SD	t-value	Remarks
Computer own	45	62.99	8.69	1.085	NS
Computer not own	53	60.84	10.9		

NS: Not Significant
S: Significant

Table 11.6: Significance Difference on the Mean Scores of Student - Teachers who were using Internet weekly and who were using Internet Monthly Awareness on 3G Technology

Category	N	Mean	SD	t-value	Remarks
Using Internet Weekly	30	63.09	8.20	0.913	NS
Using Internet Monthly	68	61.28	10.7		

NS: Not Significant
S: Significant

From Table 11.6 it is understood that the 't' value 0.066 shows that there is no significant difference at 0.05 level. These results show that the Mean Scores of Student - Teachers who were using Internet Weekly and who were using Internet Monthly with respect to the Attitude towards 3G Technology are similar. Hence the framed Null Hypothesis is accepted.

Findings

The salient findings of the study are: *(i)* All the Student - Teachers are having good Attitude towards 3G Technology. *(ii)* Male and Female, Arts and Science Student - Teachers and Student - Teachers who are having own Computer and not having own Computer and Student - Teachers who are using Internet Weekly and who are using Internet Monthly show similar level of Attitude towards 3G Technology.

Conclusions

The significant higher Attitude towards 3G Technology among Student - Teachers shows that they have awareness towards Modern Technologies. Of course it is a positive trend. This may be due to the high Literacy Rates and Media

Development. The results show that Gender, Subject, Computer ownership and frequency of Utilization Internet were not the influencing factor in determining Attitude towards 3G Technology. This is because most of the Student - Teachers were using the latest Mobiles with new Technologies. More over the Student - Teachers have awareness towards various Generations in Mobile Technology.

Education Implications

Student - Teachers have higher Attitude towards 3G Technologies thus this technology may be utilized to promote Teacher Education and School Education. Therefore the M-Learning can be implemented in the Education System. Teacher Educators should well verse with this 3G Technology because they should educate the Student - Teachers to utilize the 3G system in the correct way. The Government may issue the 3G mobile to the College Students in a concession rate so that the lower middle class students can able to purchase it. Various project works may be given the Students in relation with 3G systems which encourage the Students to use 3G Technologies regularly.

REFERENCES

Arul Sekar, J. M., Thiyagu. K. (2007). Information and Communication Technology in Education, Prophet Publishers, Tiruchirappalli.

Veena Rani, Pandy, (2008), Educational Technology Modern Perspective, (2008), Sumit Enterprises, New Delhi.

Nagarajan. K, (2006). Research Methodolgy in Education, Ram Publishers, Chennai.

Best, J. W., Research in Education, Prentice – Hall of India Pvt. Ltd., New Delhi.

Lokesh Koul. (2005). Methodology of Educational Research, Vikas Publishing House Pvt. Ltd., New Delhi.

Rama, J. M, (1997). Human Rights and Indian Values, New Delhi, NCTC.

http://www.ibimapublishing.com/journals/CIBIMA/2012/622123/622123.pdf

en.wikipedia.org/wiki/3G

3gmobile.co.in/

www.ijcte.org/papers/367-G1072.pdf

www.broadbandindia.com › Forum › My ISP/ 3G / 4G › 3G India

Page 86-90
Recent Trend in Educational Research
***Edited by:* Dr. D. Sivakumar**
***Edition:* 2015**
ISBN: 978-93-5056-741-8
***Published by:* Discovery Publishing House Pvt. Ltd., New Delhi (India)**

12

E-content Development on Flander's Interaction Analysis in Teaching of Biology at B.Ed Level

R. Rajalakshmi

INTRODUCTION

The development of Science and Technology, especially the application of information and communication technology (ICT) in the new era has greatly influenced teaching and learning in education. In the present era of knowledge explosion, adopting modern tools for teaching is one of the predominant needs of the hour. Instructional technology in the third world is changing rapidly. Knowledge packaging in electronic form or e-content is a powerful technique for teaching all subjects. ICT have become handy in classroom teaching which has the potential to engage the students throughout the period and make learning easy and effective through, visual aids, animations and simulations.

Need for the Study

New innovations are coming to the fields of education in terms of technology which promises to change the process of teaching and learning. Training of competent teachers is very important because they directly or indirectly influence

Ph.D. Scholar, Tamil University, Thanjavur.

the quality and the quantity of educational services. Without adequately trained teacher cadre the institution cannot aim to expand the educational facilities.

E-content

The term 'e-content' refers to that form of knowledge or content which is packed in an electronic form. It includes: text, audio, video, animations, images etc. An innovative application of computer in the teaching and learning process is e-content. E-content is the advancement of technology to design, deliver, select, administer and extend learning.

Objectives of the Study

1. To prepare e-content for particular topic in Teaching of Biology at B.Ed level.
2. To find out the effectiveness of e-content development in the learning process.
3. To validate the developed e-content.

Methodology

The investigator followed the experimental method for the present study. The data thus collected were put into appropriate statistical analysis: Mean, t-test, standard deviation.

Sampling Procedure

The present study is concerned only with B.Ed student teachers in J.J. College of Education and Oxford College of Education, Trichy. Hence the college selected could be considered as a representative college. Eighteen students have been selected for experimental group and another eighteen students for control group by using simple random sampling method.

Hypotheses of the Study

The following hypotheses were formulated based on the objectives of the study.

1. There is no significant difference in the mean scores of control group and experimental groups in pre-test.
2. There is no significant difference in the mean scores of control group and experimental group in post-test.
3. There is no significant difference between pre - and post-test mean scores of control group who taught by traditional lecture method.

4. There is significant difference between the pre - and post-test mean scores of experimental groups who learnt through e-content.

Hypothetical Testing

Table 12.1: Shows the Comparison of Pre-test Scores of Experimental Group and Control Group

Group Compared	N	M	SD	't' value	df	Level of Significance
Experimental Group	18	10.72	1.364	1.43	34	Not significant
Control Group	18	8.72	1.322			

The calculated t-value 1.43 is less than the critical value 2.704 corresponding to the 0.01 level of significance. This implies that the control group and experimental group don't differ significantly in their achievement in the pre-test. Hence the null hypothesis is accepted.

Table 12.2: Shows the Comparison of Post-test Scores of Experimental Group and Control Group

Group Compared	N	M	SD	't' value	df	Level of Significance
Experimental Group	18	13.33	1.910	9.22	34	Significant
Control Group	18	8.72	1.127			

The calculated t-value 9.22 is greater than the critical value 2.704 corresponding to the 0.01 level of significance. This implies that the control group and experimental group differ significantly in their achievement in the post-test. Hence the null hypothesis is rejected.

Table 12.3: Shows the Difference between the Pre-test and Post-test Scores for the Control Group

Group Compared	No of Students	Means	SD	't' value	df	Level of Significance
Pre-test	18	8.720	1.322	0.001	34	Not significant
Post-test	18	8.723	1.127			

The calculated t-value 0.001 is less than the critical value 2.021 corresponding to the 0.05 and 2.704 corresponding to the 0.01 level of significance. This implies that the pre-test and post-test control groups do not differ significantly in their achievement. Hence the null hypothesis is accepted.

Table 12.4: Shows the Difference between the Pre-test and Post-test Scores due to Treatment for the Experimental Group

Experimental Group	No of Students	Means	SD	't' value	df	Level of Significance
Pre-test	18	10.72	1.364	8.040	34	Not Significant
Post-test	18	13.33	1.910			

The calculated t-value 8.040 is less than the critical value 2.704 corresponding to the 0.01 level of significance. This pre-test and post-test of experimental group is highly significant in their achievement in post-test. Hence the hypothesis is not rejected.

Major Findings of the Study

The major findings which have emerged from the study are as follows:

1. An Achievement test was conducted for validating the developed e-content to access the effectiveness of the e-content. While analyzing the result, *i.e.*, the performance of the students in the achievement test is better and it became clear that the e-content is effective.
2. While administering the e-content to the students, which is a self-instructional learning strategy it is found that e-content promotes active participation and encourages vigilance.
3. The trainees of experimental group who were taught through e-content achieved more in subject units then the trainees at control group.
4. It was found again that learning through e-content and learning through traditional lecture method are not similar and they differ significantly.

Educational Implications of the Study

1. New instructional techniques of assisting student through computer are to be explored by the teachers and researchers continuously.

2. Teachers of higher secondary schools can be given orientation as how to develop e-content.
3. The use of e-content is found to be valid in enhancing the achievement; it will diminish wastage and stagnation in school.

Conclusion

Based on the proceeding findings of the study, the following conclusions are arrived.

The levels of performance of teacher trainees who learnt through e-content were greater the other part and hence it was evident that e-content is also an effective approach to teach Biology. The rise of e-learning and an electronic content (e-content) is a new paradigm for education and training in the knowledge society, empowered by technological advancements which give the modern instructional technology. The development of educational content in time with the changing times has become a major responsibility of the modern teacher who has to face a new learner in a new environments. More over the level of motivation, learning style and anxiety towards computer improves the efficiency of the teacher trainees and hence the e-content approach is having great scope in the instructional design of the teacher trainees.

REFERENCES

Amutha. S. and Ramganesh. E e-content – An Inevitable Supplement for a Teacher Educator. Paper presented at the *International Conference on Quality Enhancement in Distance Education for Life Long Learning* 26-27 March 2011, Edited by Dr. K. Anandhan, Bharathidasan University.

Jeya Shanmuga Raja. J, E-Content Development on Teaching method of Zoology at B.Ed Level., Paper presented at the *International Conference on Quality Enhancement in Distance Education for LifeLong Learning* 26-27 March 2011, Edited by Dr. K. Anandhan, Bharathidasan University.

Suma. S. (2007). Development and Validation of E-content on the uses of the Simple Present tense in English at Higher Secondary Level. M.Phil Thesis Submitted to Bharathidasan University.

Page 91-96
Recent Trend in Educational Research
Edited by: **Dr. D. Sivakumar**
Edition: **2015**
ISBN: 978-93-5056-741-8
Published by: **Discovery Publishing House Pvt. Ltd., New Delhi (India)**

13

A Study of Critical Thinking on Learning Style among B.Ed. Trainees

S. Subramanian and T. Yogaraj

INTRODUCTION

The student teachers receive education from B.Ed. colleges normally try to enhance the trainees performance in academic as well as non-academic. Critical thinking is self-guided, self-disciplined thinking which attempts to reason at the highest level of quality in a fair-minded way. Like wise the trainee teachers have the sense of critical thinking. They are always improve their reasoning abilities, prejudices, biases, distortions, uncritically accepted social rules and taboos, and self-interest. They strive to improve the world in whatever ways they can contribute to more rational, civilized society. For this reason, the development of critical thinking skills and dispositions influence the learning style. Learning styles are, in its simplest form, approaches or ways of learning. It involves learning methods that are presumed to allow that individual to learn best. It is commonly believed that most people favour some particular methods of interacting with, taking in, and processing stimuli or information. The idea of 'individualized learning

Ph.D. Scholars, Manonmaniam Sundaranar University, Tirnelveli.

styles' originated in the 1970s. It has gained popularity in recent years, based on this concept. It has been proposed that teachers should assess the learning styles of their students and adapt their classroom methods to fit each student's learning style.

Critical Thinking

Critical thinking is not a matter of accumulating information. A person with a good memory and who knows a lot of facts is not necessarily good at critical thinking. A critical thinker is able to deduce consequences from what he knows, and he knows how to make use of information to solve-problems, and to seek relevant sources of information to inform him self.

Learning Style

Learning styles reflect our preferred manner of acquiring, using and thinking about knowledge. It is our own way of inputting, processing, concentrating, remembering, understanding, and storing processing information. Here the investigator mentions VAK learning styles as learning style.

Significance of the Study

Learning styles reflect our preferred manner of acquiring, using, and thinking about knowledge. These styles are not abilities, but types adopted for learning. They represent the ways we approach this task. Even though our ability may be identical to someone else's, our learning styles might be quite different. All of us have preferred ways of learning, approaches that work best for him/her. And our success is not just dependent on how well we learn, but on how we learn. Our style reflects our preferences regarding which abilities you like to use not the abilities themselves. We should use our personal learning style to study more effectively. The development of critical thinking skills in students at all age levels has long been a national concern. As such, teaching faculty in all disciplines and at all levels of education shared a common goal: to develop in students in the complex mental operations that will allow them to be successful in the classroom as well as their future careers. A review of education literature reveals several factors that have been found to influence cognitive development. Learning style was one such factor. This study sought to investigate the influence of critical thinking on learning style of student teachers enrolled in the colleges of education.

Objective

To find out the level of critical thinking on learning styles among B.Ed. trainees with reference to sex.

Null Hypotheses

Suitable null hypotheses were framed.

Methodology

The researcher has used the survey method for obtaining the data.

Sample for the Study

The investigator has randomly selected 239 B.Ed. trainees from Tirunelveli, Districts.

Tool Used

The researcher adopted the critical thinking (Rani and Porgio 2010) and learning style inventories (Arockiyasamy and Lawrence 2009) for the collection of data.

Statistical Techniques Used

SD, t-test and ANOVA used for analysis of the data.

Table 13.1: Level of Critical Thinking on Learning Style among BEd. Trainees

Dimensions	Male						Female					
	Low		Average		High		Low		Average		High	
	N	%	N	%	N	%	N	%	N	%	N	%
Dispositions	16	15.7	69	67.6	17	16.7	24	17.4	92	66.7	22	15.9
Problem-solving	11	10.8	72	70.6	19	18.6	23	16.7	91	65.9	24	17.4
Decision-making	18	17.6	66	64.7	18	17.6	14	10.1	103	74.6	21	15.2
Visual	17	16.7	72	70.6	13	12.7	23	16.7	90	65.2	25	18.1
Auditory	13	12.7	80	78.4	9	8.8	26	18.8	90	65.2	22	15.9
Kinesthetic	17	16.7	69	67.6	16	15.7	26	18.8	88	63.8	24	17.4

Regarding male B.Ed. trainees 15.7 per cent, 10.8 per cent, 17.6 per cent, 16.7 per cent 12.7 per cent 16.7 per cent, of them have low level, 67.6 per cent, 70.6 per cent, 64.7 per cent, 70.6 per cent, 78.4 per cent 67.6 per cent, of them have average level, 16.7 per cent, 18.6 per cent, 17.6 per cent, 12.7 per cent, 8.8 per cent, 15.7 per cent of them have high level of critical thinking on learning style of B.Ed. trainees. Regarding female B.Ed. trainees 17.4 per cent, 16.7 per cent, 10.1 per cent, 16.7 per cent, 18.8 per cent, 18.8 per cent, of them have low level, 66.7 per cent, 65.9 per cent, 74.6 per cent, 65.2 per cent, 65.2 per cent, 63.8 per cent them have average level and 15.9 per cent, 17.4 per cent, 15.2 per cent, 18.1 per cent, 15.9 per cent, 17.4 per cent of them have high level of critical thinking on learning style of B.Ed. trainees.

Null Hypothesis

There is no significant difference between critical thinking on learning style among B.Ed. trainees with reference to sex.

Table 13.2: Difference between Critical Thinking on Learning Style among B.Ed. Trainees with Reference to Sex

Dimensions	Male		Female		Calculated 't' value Remarks	Remarks
	Mean	S.D	Mean	S.D		
Dispositions	48.31	9.82	51.25	9.99	2.27	S
Problem-solving	50.26	9.50	49.81	10.38	0.34	NS
Decision-making	48.91	10.18	50.80	9.82	1.44	NS
Visual	49.48	9.50	50.38	10.37	0.70	NS
Auditory	49.18	10.80	50.60	9.36	1.07	NS
Kinesthetic	48.82	9.93	50.88	10.00	1.58	NS

(At 5% level of significance, the table value of 't' is 1.96)

It is inferred from Table 13.2 that there is no significant difference between male and female B.Ed. trainees in the dimensions of critical thinking on learning style towards problem-solving, decision-making, visual, auditory and kinesthetic but there is significant difference between male and female B.Ed. trainees in disposition critical thinking on learning style.

Null Hypothesis

There is no significant difference among critical thinking on learning style with reference to parents educational qualification.

Table 13.3: Difference among Critical Thinking on Learning Style with Reference to Parents Educational Qualification

Dimensions	Source of Variation	Sum of Squares	Variance Estimate	Calculated Value of 'F'	Remarks
Dispositions	Between	215.70	107.85	1.08	NS
	Within	23684.30	99.93		
Problem-solving	Between	515.46	257.73	2.61	NS
	Within	23384.54	98.67		
Decision-making	Between	277.06	138.53	1.39	NS
	Within	23622.94	99.67		
Visual	Between	538.11	269.05	2.73	NS
	Within	23361.89	98.57		
Auditory	Between	294.03	147.01	1.48	NS
	Within	23605.97	99.60		
Kinesthetic	Between	493.84	246.92	2.50	NS
	Within	23406.16	98.76		

(At 5% level of significance for 2, 237 df the table value of 'F' is 3.03)

It is inferred from Table 13.3 that there is no significant difference among the parents educational qualification such as degree, post-graduate and technical qualification of critical thinking on learning style of B.Ed. trainees and its dimensions.

Findings

- The percentage level found out the critical thinking on learning style among B.Ed. trainees the female B.Ed. trainees are having high per cent of average performance more than male B.Ed. trainees.
- There is a significant difference between male and female B.Ed. trainees in their dimension of disposition of their critical thinking on learning style among B.Ed. trainees.
- There is no significant difference male and female B.Ed. trainees in their dimensions of problem-solving, decision-

making, visual, auditory and kinesthetic of their critical thinking on learning stye among B.Ed. trainees.

- There is no significant difference among critical thinking on learning style with reference to parents educational qualification of degree, post-graduate and technical qualification.

Recommendations

- Seminars should be conducted for student teacher in order to raise the level of creating awareness of critical thinking and learning style.
- The female trainees having high level of critical thinking on learning style more than male trainees. So try to enhance the quality of male trainees through proper training.
- A small project work on critical thinking and testing the learning style through teaching competency should be given to student teachers in order to help them to understand their problems.

REFERENCES

Arora R.K., (1992). Interactional Effect of Creating Intelligence on Emotional Stability, Personality Adjustment and Academic Achievement, *Indian Educational Review*, Vol. 27, No. 4, p. 86-93.

Ennis, Robert H. (2011a). Critical Thinking: Reflection And Perspective-Part I. Inquiry, Vol. 26, 1.

Ennis, Robert H. (2011b). Defending Sole Singular Causal Claims. In Zenker, Frank (ed.). Argumentation: Cognition and Community. Proceedings of the 9th International Conference of the Ontario Society for the Study of Argumentation (OSSA), May 18-21, 2011.

Page 97-103

Recent Trend in Educational Research
Edited by: **Dr. D. Sivakumar**
Edition: **2015**
ISBN: 978-93-5056-741-8
Published by: **Discovery Publishing House Pvt. Ltd., New Delhi (India)**

14

A Study on Thinking Styles of B.Ed. Student Teachers

A. Balamallikadevi

INTRODUCTION

'How do people think about things?' Harrison and Bramson, through their research detailed in their text The Art of Thinking, found that there are five distinct styles of thinking. Most people show a marked preference for one or two of the styles. These styles are referred to as 'inquiry Modes.' The Art of Thinking by Allen Harrison and Robert Bramson provides much information about the different way that people think and they are:

- The Synthesist - sees likeness in apparent unlike, sees conflict, interested in change.
- The Idealist - welcomes a broad range of views, seeks ideal solutions.
- The Pragmatist - 'whatever works' - seeks shortest route to payoff.
- The Analyst - seeks one 'best way', interested in scientific solutions.

Ph.D. Research Scholar, Sri Sarada College of Education, (Autonomous) Salem - 16.

- The Realist - relies on facts and expert opinions, interested in concrete results.

"Synthesists are apt to appear challenging, skeptical (disbelieving), or satirically (sarcastically) amused, even when they can see no cause for any of that." They may find them difficult because they tend to enjoy conflict and argument simply for the sake of argument. A Synthesist can juggle both arguments and counter arguments mentally and recognize the validity of each and form new ideas from that conflict. The first common strategy of the Synthesist is that of 'Open Argument and Confrontation.' Synthesists realize that this fires creativity. They will openly confront antagonists and appear aggressive or abrasive. Their second common strategy is 'Asking Dumb-Smart Questions.' This means that they will often, ask a question to which they already know the answer in order to get the respondent to open up.

Statement of the Study

The statement of the present study is 'A Study on Thinking Styles of B.Ed. Student Teachers'.

Objectives of the Study

- To find the thinking styles of B.Ed. students teachers.
- To analyse The Thinking Styles of Student Teachers of different disciplines Such as: Tamil, English, Mathematics, Physical Science, Biological Science and History.
- To study the dominant thinking style and the combination of thinking styles of the student teachers.

Methodology

The study was based on a normative survey method. The tool used for the study was an standardized online tool prepared by Harrison and Bramson to assess the five types thinking styles as: *(i)* synthesist; *(ii)* analyst; *(iii)* realist; *(iv)* idealist; and *(v)* pragmatist. The tool consists of 18 statements in which each statement has five options and each option support one style of thinking. The scoring was done through online and the percentage was found. The sample of the study was the student teachers of B.Ed. from different disciplines and the sample consist of 30 students.

Analysis and Interpretation

Table 14.1: Shows the Percentage Score of Tamil and Tamil Students

Students	Synthesist	Idealist	Pragmatist	Analyst	Realist
1.	55%	64%	45%	53%	35%
2.	49%	46%	42%	61%	54%
3.	45%	46%	64%	46%	52%
4.	39%	58%	44%	54%	57%
5.	52%	63%	47%	42%	48%

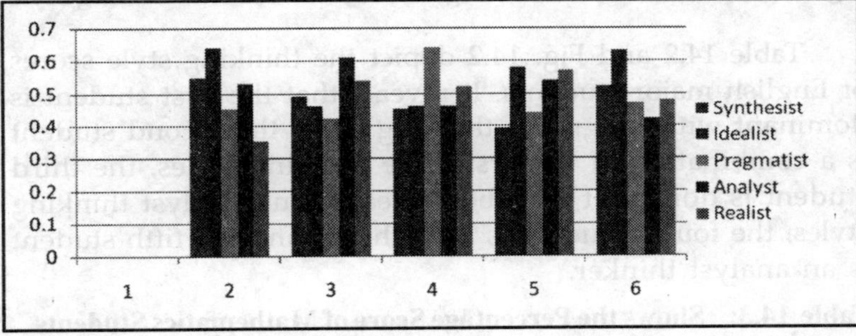

Fig. 14.1:

From Table 14.1 and Fig. 14.2 the different types of thinking of the B.Ed. Tamil major students are given. Among the five students four of them have scored more in any one of the thinking styles as first and the fourth student are dominated with idealist thinking style, the second student is an analyst thinker, while the third student is dominant with pragmatic thinking style and the fifth student is an idealist thinker. But the fourth student has scored more or less equally in all the five skills. If any individual have scored equally he is a versatile thinker.

Table 14.2: Shows the Percentage Score of English and English Students

Students	Synthesist	Idealist	Pragmatist	Analyst	Realist
1.	54%	45%	63%	48%	42%
2.	51%	55%	56%	43%	47%
3.	46%	61%	40%	62%	43%
4.	63%	43%	53%	49%	44%
5.	44%	59%	42%	64%	43%

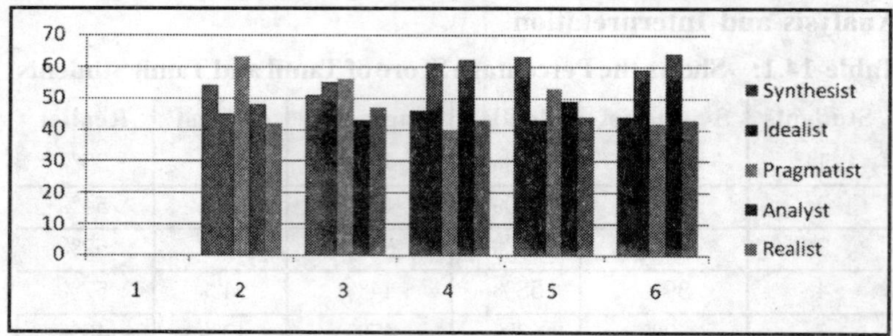

Fig. 14.2: Shows the Scores of English Major Students Thinking Style

Table 14.2 and Fig. 14.2 depict the thinking style scores of English major students. It reveals that the first student is dominant with pragmatic thinking style, the second student is a combination of the first three thinking styles, the third student is dominant with both idealist and analyst thinking styles, the fourth student is a synthesist and the fifth student is an analyst thinker.

Table 14.3: Shows the Percentage Score of Mathematics Students

Students	Synthesist	Idealist	Pragmatist	Analyst	Realist
1.	54%	52%	40%	42%	64%
2.	47%	52%	61%	44%	48%
3.	56%	65%	41%	47%	43%
4.	40%	64%	49%	53%	46%
5.	54%	52%	40%	42%	64%

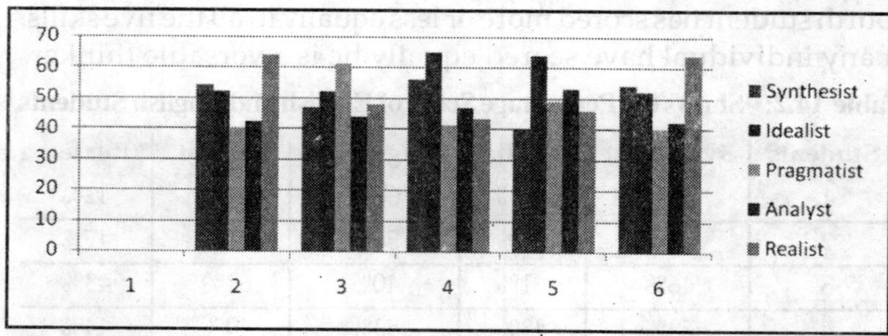

Fig. 14.3: Shows the Scores of Mathematics Students Thinking Style

While considering Table 14.3 it displays the percentage scores of mathematics students, and the figure it is clear that the first and fifth student is dominated with realist thinking styles, the third and fourth students are dominated with idealist thinking styles, and the second student is a pragmatist thinker.

Table 14.4: Shows the Percentage Score of Physical Science Students

Students	Synthesist	Idealist	Pragmatist	Analyst	Realist
1.	52%	55%	38%	63%	44%
2.	55%	58%	62%	42%	35%
3.	43%	56%	63%	56%	34%
4.	43%	63%	54%	44%	48%
5.	54%	52%	42%	40%	64%

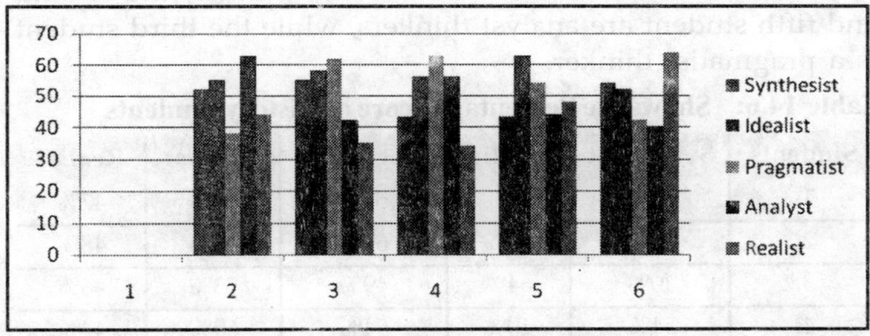

Fig. 14.4: Shows the Scores of Physical Science Students Thinking Style

Table 14.4 and the Fig. 14.4 shows the scores of physical science students. It reveals that the first student is an analyst while the second and third students are pragmatist. The fourth student is an idealist dominated thinker. The fifth student is a combination of synthesist and idealist thinking style.

Table 14.5: Shows the Percentage Score of Biological Science Students

Students	Synthesist	Idealist	Pragmatist	Analyst	Realist
1.	43%	61%	42%	44%	62%
2.	52%	53%	41%	61%	45%
3.	46%	51%	60%	47%	48%
4.	56%	48%	43%	41%	64%
5.	40%	57%	38%	65%	52%

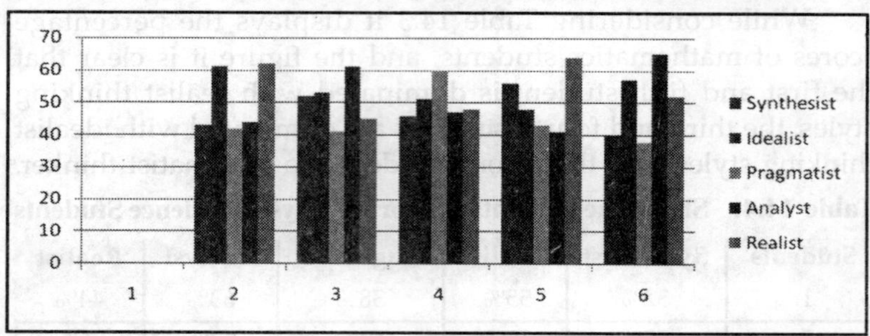

Fig. 14.5: Shows the Scores of Biological Science Students Thinking Style

Table 14.5 and Fig. 14.5 shows the biological science students scores, from which it was found that the first student is a combination of idealist and realist thinker, the second and fifth student are analyst thinkers, while the third student is a pragmatist thinker.

Table 14.6: Shows the Percentage Score of History Students

Students	Synthesist	Idealist	Pragmatist	Analyst	Realist
1.	51%	55%	56%	43%	47%
2.	47%	52%	61%	44%	48%
3.	40%	64%	49%	53%	46%
4.	54%	40%	54%	60%	44%
5.	52%	40%	58%	58%	44%

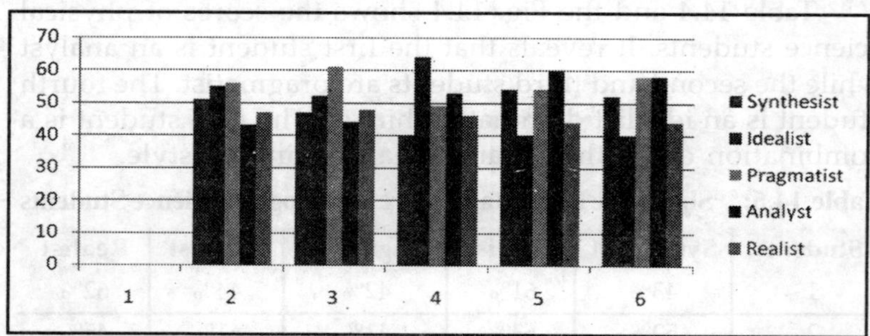

Fig. 14.6: Shows the Scores of History Students Thinking Style

While considering Table 14.6 and the Fig. 14.6 the thinking style of History students is depicted. It shows that the first student is a combination of synthesist, idealist and pragmatist thinking styles. The second student is a pragmatist dominated thinking style while third student is an idealist thinker. The fourth and the fifth students are a combination of synthesist, pragmatist and analyst thinking style.

Main Findings of the Study

1. Scores of 60 or higher on any category indicate a peak or preference for that thinking style.
2. Scores of 48 or below indicate a valley or relative disregard for that thinking style.
3. Synthesist are integrators. In a group discussion they are likely to champion an opposite point of view and are therefore valuable in avoiding 'group think'. They tend to be creative people.
4. Idealist takes a broad, holistic view of things, tending to be future oriented and to think about goals. They are interested in social values.
5. Pragmatist has a bias for action. They like to get things done and approach is often flexible and adaptive. The model of pragmatist is 'whatever works'.
6. Analyst tends to be logical, structured and prescriptive. They prefer predictability and rationality and will look for a method, a formula, or procedure to solve a particular problem. They believe that there is 'one best way' to solve any problem.
7. Realist takes an empirical view. Their world consists of what can be felt, seen, personally observed or experienced. They are interested in concrete results and at times may appear to be too result oriented.

Conclusion

Generally about half of any population would be expected to have a peak in a single thinking 35 per cent of people will have peaks in two thinking styles, with the most common combinations being analyst/realist, idealist/analyst, and synthesist and idealist. The rarest combination is synthesist and realist. 2 per cent of general population has a preference for three styles.

Page 104-108
Recent Trend in Educational Research
Edited by: **Dr. D. Sivakumar**
Edition: **2015**
ISBN: 978-93-5056-741-8
Published by: **Discovery Publishing House Pvt. Ltd., New Delhi (India)**

15

Comparison of Value Pattern among Secondary and Higher Secondary Students

K. Subashini

INTRODUCTION

The nucleus of human perfection, the convergence of cultural achievements, the sunstone and quintessence of refinement owe their origin to education. Education is the strong instrument to attain national goals – a united secular India, a modern nation, a productive people and a humane and caring society. A central goal of education is to develop the ability to think and reason. Education for development of values is mostly neglected in our schools and colleges. In our present system the cognitive domain is developed to some extent, but the effective value internationalization and character building are missing. In addition to technological advancement, there has been a revolutionary change in the field of values, due to the influence of western culture industrialization, modernization, urbanization and other international transactions.

Need for the Present Study

The nations of the world are striving their utmost to bring in to the lives of their people the marvels of science and

P.hD. Scholar, Sri Sarada College of Education, Salem.

technology. Indeed human life on this planet has greatly enriched with incredible technological advances. There is great anxiety that our scintillating progress in controlling and adopting our material world has not been matched by corresponding advance in human character and virtue. Indeed, many observers feel that more values are disintegrating in all walks of life, both public and personal. Today due to the advancement of science and technology, life has become so sophisticated and very simple. Due to the magnificent advancement in technology, life has become very simple; there is hardly anything to work with labour. Everything is performed by machines and latest modalities. If the younger siblings are rich in their value system, then the home itself is beautiful reflect in school, nation and world itself, there the need is felt to compare the value pattern among secondary and higher secondary students.

Statement of the Problem

'To compare the value pattern among secondary and higher secondary students'.

Objectives

1. To study the value pattern followed by boys of secondary and higher secondary level.
2. To know the value pattern adopted by girls of secondary and higher secondary level.
3. To find the value pattern adhered by students of secondary and higher secondary level.

Tool

A situational test was administered. It consisted of situations, which were selected from the list that has been compiled on the basis of the documents included in the publication by NCERT. 20 situations formed for each value. Likewise 60 situations formed for 3 values. The test was administered in English. Each choice suggested a response to the given situations; the responses were in positive, negative and neutral types. The tool was standardized.

Sample

A sample of 300 boys and girls of secondary and higher secondary students of Chennai were randomly selected for the study. 150 boys and 150 girls were selected.

Hypothesis

1. There would be no significant difference in the values followed by boys among secondary and higher secondary level students.
2. There would be no significant difference in the values adopted by girls among secondary and higher secondary level students.
3. There would be no significant difference in the values adhered by secondary and higher secondary level students.

Statistical Analysis

Mean, Standard deviation, t-value have been calculated.

Analysis and Discussion

Table 15.1: Mean, Standard Deviation, T-value of the Scores for the Value of 'Truth' of Boys and Girls at Secondary and Higher Secondary Level

Gender	Variable	N	Mean	SD	t-value	Level of Significance
Boys	Secondary level	75	26.72	7.26	6.714	Significant at 0.01 level
Boys	Higher secondary level	75	33.28	7.94		
Girls	Secondary level	75	47.76	5.136	3.85	Significant at 0.01 level
Girls	Higher secondary level	75	44.49	5.236		

From Table 15.1 it is evident that higher secondary boys were comparatively better than the secondary school boys in the value of Truth. The table also reveals that secondary school girls have better value of truth than higher secondary school girls.

Table 15.2: Mean, Standard Deviation, T-value of the Scores for the Value of 'Right Conduct' of Boys and Girls at Secondary and Higher Secondary Level

Gender	Variable	N	Mean	SD	t-value	Level of Significance
Boys	Secondary level	75	30.24	7.64	3.38	Significant at 0.01 level
Boys	Higher secondary level	75	26.25	6.78		
Girls	Secondary level	75	47.58	7.58	4.61	Significant at 0.01 level
Girls	Higher secondary level	75	52.10	5.62		

This Table 15.2 indicates that Secondary School boys were better than the Higher Secondary School boys in the value right conduct. And also Higher Secondary School Girls were better the value of right conduct than the Secondary School Girls.

Table 15.3: Mean, Standard Deviation, T-value of the Scores for the Value of 'Sense of Responsibility' of Boys and Girls at Secondary and Higher Secondary Level

Gender	Variable	N	Mean	SD	t-value	Level of Significance
Boys	Secondary level	75	26.24	7.82	8.89	Significant at 0.01 level
Boys	Higher secondary level	75	36.78	6.13		
Girls	Secondary level	75	49.80	5.41	3.72	Significant at 0.01 level
Girls	Higher secondary level	75	53.10	5.46		

Table 15.3 shows that Higher Secondary School boys and Girls have better value of Sense of Responsibility than Secondary School boys and girls.

Table 15.4: Mean, Standard Deviation, T-value of the Scores for the Values of Boys and Girls at Secondary and Higher Secondary Level

Gender	Variable	N	Mean	SD	t-value	Level of Significance
Boys	Secondary level	75	26.62	12.67	10.62	Significant at 0.01 level
Boys	Higher secondary level	75	3.89	13.54		
Girls	Secondary level	75	74.40	11.49	45.56	Significant at 0.01 level
Girls	Higher secondary level	75	20.90	13.02		

Table 15.4 indicates that Secondary School boys have better value pattern than Higher Secondary School Boys. The Higher Secondary School girls have better value pattern than Secondary school girls.

Findings

- Higher Secondary School boys were comparatively better in the value of Truth and sense of responsibility than secondary school boys.
- Secondary school boys were better in the value of right conduct than Higher Secondary Boys.

- Higher Secondary School girls were better in the value of right conduct and responsibility than secondary school girls.
- Secondary school girls were better in the value of 'Truth' than Higher Secondary School girls.
- Secondary School boys have better value pattern than Higher Secondary School Boys. The Higher Secondary School girls have better value pattern than Secondary school girls.

Educational Implication

Today, since the mind of the people have polluted, so there is pollution in the entire world. This pollution of mind is due to the cause of destruction of values which is inherited in our culture of Bharat.

'Bharat' which is full of values and culture have taken the first place and guiding the whole world in a right path. Bharat is called 'Karma Bhoomi, Janana Bhoomi'. Values are present in every nook and corner of our country. Even the dust of our land has truth.

In ancient times, those people followed the Gurukula system of education. Their aim was to impart education which is for life itself. As the saying goes, 'Education is not for mere living, Education is for life itself'.

REFERENCES

Bavani, Devi. R., "Teacher's Perception about the Role of Parents for Inculcation of Values among Children – A Synthesized Overview," *Journal of Humanities and Social Sciences*, 2009.

Best John, Research in Education, New Delhi, 1990.

Chakrabarty, S.K. "Values in our Lives", A Pilot Study, Vivekananda Nidhi, Calcutta, 1989.

Chilana, M.R., Dhawan, M.L., "The Human Values" A Task for all, Concept Publication, New Delhi 1998.

Dhankar Neerja, "Value Education in Schools" A.P.H. Publishing Corporation, New Delhi 2010.

Harim, M.H. Kirschenbaum and S.B. Simon, "Carifying Values through Subject Matter. Minneapolis Winston Press 1973.

Joshi Dhananjay, "Value Education in Global Perspective" Lotus Press, New Delhi 2006.

Page 109-113
Recent Trend in Educational Research
***Edited by:* Dr. D. Sivakumar**
***Edition:* 2015**
ISBN: 978-93-5056-741-8
***Published by:* Discovery Publishing House Pvt. Ltd., New Delhi (India)**

16

Problems faced by Principals in Implementing Training for Web-based Instruction

S. Vimala Ramani

INTRODUCTION

The World Wide Web can be used to provide instruction and instructional support. Web-based instruction offers learners unparalleled access to instructional resources, far surpassing the reach of the traditional classroom. It also makes possible learning experiences that are open, flexible, and distributed, providing opportunities for engaging, interactive, and efficient instruction Web-based instruction offers multiple dimensions of use in education and training environments. The Web has become a powerful tool for learning and teaching at a distance. Its inherent flexibility allows application in a variety of ways within an educational context, ranging from simple course administration and student management to teaching entire courses online. Each of these types of use works towards a different goal. These goals should be recognized when evaluating the use of the Web.

Web-based training (WBT) is an innovative approach to distance learning in which computer-based training (CBT) is

Ph.D. Scholar, Sri Sarada College of Education, Salem - 16. Tamil Nadu.

transformed by the technologies and methodologies of the World Wide Web, the Internet, and intranets. Web-based training presents live content, as fresh as the moment and modified at will, in a structure allowing self-directed, self-paced instruction in any topic. WBT is media-rich training fully capable of evaluation, adaptation, and remediation, all independent of computer platform.

Need for the Study

Teachers must transact school curriculum to the students in the best method. At this present scenario web-based education is the best technology. To make use of this method, they must be properly trained. For implementing such WBI training for the teachers, the principals of the school may face some problems. So the investigator wants to analyze the problems faced by principals in implementing web-based training.

Objectives

The following are the main objectives of the study.

1. To find the level of problems given by the teaching staff, non-teaching staff, Parents and Students.
2. To find the level of problems with their type of school, Gender, experience, type of family and marital status.

Method

Purposive sampling technique was used to gather data from the principals.

Sample

In, this study 30 principals are taken as samples in Salem district.

Tool used for the Study

The tool is prepared by the investigator. The tool consist of 20 items out of which 5 items for teaching staff, 5 items for non-teaching staff, 5 for parents and 5 for students. The tool was standardized by conducting pilot study by following the test and retest method. The calculate value is higher than the table value, so the tool was reliable for the sample. Content validity was done for validation of the tool.

Analysis and Interpretation

Table 16.1: Shows the Percentage of Problems

S. No.	Problems	Percentage (%)
1.	Teaching staff	82.2%
2.	Non teaching staff	46.32%
3.	Parents	58.68%
4.	Students	23.2%

The Principals faced maximum level of problems with their teaching staff while implementing the training for Web based Instruction in schools.

Table 16.2: It Shows the Mean and Standard Deviation Related to their Type of School

Variables		N	M	S.D	t-value
Type of School	Government	12	75.50	4.46	2.3048*
	Government Aided	11	80.82	7.55	
	Government	12	75.50	4.46	8.3736*
	Private	7	91.71	3.77	
	Government Aided	11	83.45	2.84	6.6552*
	Private	7	92.57	2.82	

*Significant ** Not significant

The government aided school principals face problems in implementing training for web-based instruction than the government school principals. The government school principals face problems in implementing training for web-based instruction than the private school principals. The government school principals face problems in implementing training for web-based instruction than the private school principals.

When compared to the principals gender, the mean score of male is higher than the women. The mean score of below 15 years experienced principals is higher than above 15 years experienced principals. When compared to the marital status, the mean score of unmarried principals is higher than that of married principals. When compared to the type of family the mean score of nuclear family principals is higher than the joint family principals.

Table 16.3: It Shows the Mean and Standard Deviation of Principals

Variables		N	M	S.D	t-value
Gender	Male	14	80	3.98	4.1394*
	Female	16	74	4.10	
Experience	Below 15	16	81.56	2.68	6.7369*
	Above 15	14	73.62	3.84	
Marital Status	Married	23	79.52	8.03	3.4417*
	Unmarried	7	90.71	5.31	
Family	Joint	18	78.33	8.07	2.8437*
	Nuclear	12	86.42	6.89	

*Significant, **Not significant

Findings of the Study

- The government aided school principals face problems in implementing training for web-based instruction than the government school principals.
- The government school principals face problems in implementing training for web-based instruction than the private school principals.
- The government school principals face problems in implementing training for web-based instruction than the private school principals.
- The male principals face problems in implementing training for web-based instruction than the female principals.
- The below 15 years experienced principals face problems in implementing training for web-based instruction than the above 15 years experienced principals.
- The nuclear family principals face problems in implementing training for web-based instruction than the joint family principals.
- The unmarried principals face problems in implementing training for web-based instruction than the married principals

Conclusion

When implementing Web-based instruction into the curriculum, it is essential to consider carefully the implications for faculty and student development needs so that the technology can be efficiently and effectively used to support student learning. Teaching a Web-based course is a new experience for many faculties and requires a reconceptualization of the faculty role. Faculty issues to consider when implementing Web-based instruction include instructional design concerns, faculty-student interactions, time and technology management skills, and student outcome evaluation. Students, especially those who have a preference for faculty-directed classroom learning, also will find student role challenges in Web-based learning.

REFERENCES

Angulo, A. J., and Bruce, M. (1999). Student Perceptions of Supplemental Web-based Instruction. *Innovative Higher Education*, 24, 105-125.

Arvan, L., Ory, J. C., Bullock, C. D., Burnaska, K. K., and Hanson, M. (1998). The SCALE Efficiency Projects. *Journal of Asynchronous Learning Networks*, 2, 33-60.

Banta, T. W., Lund, J. P., Black, K. E., and Oblander, F. W. (1996). *Assessment in Practice: Putting Principles to Work on College Campuses*. San Francisco: Jossey-Bass.

Black, P., and William, D. (1998b). Inside the Black Box: Raising Standards through Classroom Assessment. *Phi Delta Kappan*, 80 (2): 139-148.

Chickering, A.W., and Ehrmann, S.C. (1996). Implementing the Seven Principles: Technology as Lever. *American Association for Higher Education Bulletin*, 3-6.

Dills, C., and Romiszowski, A. J. (1997). *Instructional Development Paradigms*. Englewood Cliffs, NJ.: Educational Technology Publications.

Fletcher, J. D. (1990). *Effectiveness and Cost of Interactive Videodisc Instruction in Defense Training and Education*. Institute for Defense Analyses Paper p. 2372.

Page 114-119
Recent Trend in Educational Research
Edited by: **Dr. D. Sivakumar**
Edition: **2015**
ISBN: 978-93-5056-741-8
Published by: **Discovery Publishing House Pvt. Ltd., New Delhi (India)**

17

Student Teachers' Evaluation of Teacher Education Programme

Dr. (Mrs). P. Nithila Devakarunyam

INTRODUCTION

Any change implemented in any educational programme with an intention of improving its quality should be followed by evaluation. The term 'Evaluation' refers to the process of determining the merit, quality or value of entities. Since lots of changes have been made in the teacher education programme, evaluation is necessary to see the impact of those changes. Especially the effect of the teacher education programmes on the knowledge, skills and dispositions of the student teachers should be checked frequently in order to have a clear idea of the status of those programmes. Programme evaluation is carefully collecting information about a programme or some aspect of a programme in order to make necessary decisions about the programme. Programme evaluation is done to identify the strengths and weaknesses of the programme, check whether the goals of the programme are met and to make necessary modifications in the programme.

Assistant Professor in Physical Science, St. Christopher's College of Education, Chennai.

Review of Related Literature

'Effectiveness of teacher training programmes in the colleges affiliated to Avadh University, Faizabad' was a study conducted by Mohan. K, in the year 1980. The finding of the study was, majority of the respondents were not satisfied with the programmes. Sinha. P conducted 'An evaluation study of teacher education in Bihar' in 1982. The major finding was, the recent innovations in the field of teacher education had not been incorporated in to the system of teacher education in Bihar. 'Evaluation of the teacher education programme of Agra University' was done by Devi Laxmi in 1988. The major finding was that the teacher education programme did not contribute towards the teacher attitude of the student teachers. 'A study of students' perceptions about the status of teachers in Missouri' done by Larry Joe in University of Arkansas in 1990 revealed that girls had a more positive attitude towards teaching profession than boys.

Need for the Study

The quality of classroom teaching in the schools depends upon the quality of education of teachers. The quality of education of teachers depends upon the knowledge of subject matter on one hand and knowledge of pedagogy on the other hand. The knowledge of pedagogy and its application to day-to-day classroom teaching depends on the knowledge and skills acquired by the student teachers during their B.Ed. programme. Hence the knowledge acquired by them and the skills developed in them during their B.Ed. programme should be evaluated.

For each and every programme we have a set of objectives to be realized at the end of instruction. Likewise teacher education also has a list of objectives to be achieved. Any programme is good if and only if its objectives are achieved. If we want to evaluate the effectiveness of teacher education programme, we have to find out what kind of questions the student teachers can answer, what kind of attitudinal changes are produced in them and what kind of competencies are developed in them because of the teacher education programme. Then only we can find out whether the objectives of teacher education programme are attained. As the researcher felt that evaluation of the present teacher education programme would indicate its strengths and weaknesses which will help in planning appropriate remedial measures, this topic was selected for the present study.

Statement of the Problem

Student Teachers' Evaluation of Teacher Education Programme.

Objectives

1. To find out whether there is any significant difference between male and female student teachers in their evaluation of teacher education programme.
2. To find out whether there is any significant difference between student teachers studying in government and private colleges in their evaluation of teacher education programme.
3. To find out whether there is any significant difference between student teachers belonging to science and arts groups in their evaluation of teacher education programme.
4. To find out whether there is any significant difference between student teachers studying in autonomous and non-autonomous colleges in their evaluation of teacher education programme.

Hypotheses

1. There is no significant difference between male and female student teachers in their evaluation of teacher education programme.
2. There is no significant difference between student teachers studying in government and private colleges in their evaluation of teacher education programme.
3. There is no significant difference between student teachers belonging to science and arts groups in their evaluation of teacher education programme.
4. There is no significant difference between student teachers studying in autonomous and non-autonomous colleges in their evaluation of teacher education programme.

Tool Construction

The researcher had decided to prepare a rating scale since it is the most suitable tool for programme evaluation. The rating scale consisted of 45 statements. The opinion of experienced teacher educators was obtained and necessary changes have been made in the tool. In order to improve the quality of the tool three pilot studies were conducted and the necessary modifications were made in the tool. Test-retest method was used to find out the reliability of the tool. The reliability co-efficient of the tool was 0.869. The validity co-efficient of the tool was found to be 0.9322.

Methodology

Survey method was used in the study. The sample consisted of student teachers from three autonomous colleges and eleven colleges affiliated to various universities in Tamil Nadu. The sample consisted of 90 student teachers from each college. Thus the sample consisted of 1260 student teachers. The sample consisted of 690 female student teachers and 570 male student teachers. In the sample there were 720 student teachers from private colleges and 540 from Government colleges. In the total sample of 1260 student teachers, 270 were from autonomous colleges and 990 were from non-autonomous colleges.

Analysis

Table 17.1: Difference between Male and Female Student Teachers in their Evaluation of Teacher Education Programme

Gender	N	Mean	S.D	t-value	Significance Value
Male	570	171.5947	23.08361	0.908	0.364
Female	690	172.8058	23.94266		

The significance value is greater than 0.05, hence the null hypothesis is accepted. There is no significant difference between male and female student teachers in their evaluation of teacher education programme.

Table 17.2: Difference between Student Teachers Studying in Government and Private Colleges in their Evaluation of Teacher Education Programme

Type	N	Mean	S.D	t-value	Significance Value
Government	540	172.4426	19.82845	0.25	0.802
Private	720	172.1194	26.01678		

The significance value is greater than 0.05, hence the null hypothesis is accepted. There is no significant difference between student teachers studying in government and private colleges in their evaluation of teacher education programme.

Table 17.3: Difference between Student Teachers Belonging to Science and Arts Groups in their Evaluation of Teacher Education Programme

Group	N	Mean	S.D	t-value	Significance Value
Science	904	171.698	24.43656	1.432	0.152
Arts	356	173.6798	21.12308		

The significance value is greater than 0.05, hence the null hypothesis is accepted. There is no significant difference between student teachers belonging to science and arts groups in their evaluation of teacher education programme.

Table 17.4: Difference between Student Teachers Studying in Autonomous and Non-autonomous Colleges in their Evaluation of Teacher Education Programme

Status of Institution	N	Mean	S.D	t-value	Significance Value
Autonomous	270	177.7444	20.96353	4.348	0.00
Non-Autonomous	990	170.7616	24.00833		

The significance value is less than 0.05, hence the null hypothesis is rejected. There is significant difference between student teachers studying in autonomous and non-autonomous colleges in their evaluation of teacher education programme.

Major Findings

- There is no significant difference between men and women in their evaluation of the B.Ed. programme.
- There is no significant difference between student teachers studying in government and private colleges in their evaluation of the B.Ed. programme.
- There is no significant difference between student teachers belonging to science and arts groups in their evaluation.
- There is significant difference between student teachers studying in autonomous colleges and non-autonomous colleges in their evaluation. The mean evaluation score of student teachers from autonomous colleges was higher than that of student teachers from non-autonomous colleges.

Conclusion

The study revealed that the status of institution has a significant influence on the evaluation of student teachers. This may be due to the freedom autonomous colleges have in planning a variety of activities to enrich the experiences of learners.

REFERENCES

Khosla D. N, (Ed), Competency based and Commitment Oriented Teacher Education for Quality School Education - NCTE – 1998.

Kundu C. L., Indian Year Book on Teacher Education, Sterling Publishers Private Limited, New Delhi - 1988.

Michael J. Dunkin, The International Encyclopedia of Teaching and Teacher Education, Pergamon Book Ltd., England, 1987.

Robert D. Coursey (Ed), Programme Evaluation for Mental Health, Grune and Stratton, Inc, 1977.

Singh, R. P. and Gopal Rana, Teacher Education in Turmoil, Quest for a Solution - Edited by Sterling Publishers Privated Limited, New Delhi - 2002.

Talawar. M. S. (Ed), Teacher Education and Globalization, Cauvery Prakashana, Bangalore, 2005.

Page 120-124
Recent Trend in Educational Research
Edited by: **Dr. D. Sivakumar**
Edition: **2015**
ISBN: 978-93-5056-741-8
Published by: **Discovery Publishing House Pvt. Ltd., New Delhi (India)**

18

Self Awareness and Interpersonal Relationship Skills of Disabled Children in Inclusive Education Programme

S. Priyadharsini

INTRODUCTION

Life skill is a learned ability to do something well. Life skills are abilities, individuals can learn that will help them to live a fruitful life. Skills that help an individual be successful in living a productive and satisfying life (Hendricks, 1996). Self awareness is our ability to know ourselves: our character, desires, likes, dislikes and our strengths and weaknesses keeping in mind our physical, mental, emotional, social and sexual aspects. Having this skill makes us aware of our strengths and weaknesses and will help in building our self-esteem and self-confidence. Interpersonal relationship skills help the children to enhance their relationships with other people. If we look at ourselves, we will notice that we have relationships with our family, friends, in school, within communities etc., and all these are different kinds of relationships and the expectations from each are different. It is believed that this sense of wellness promotes exploration and comfort, as well as social, emotional and academic competence among students. Inclusive education

Ph.D. Research Scholar, Sri Sarada College of Education, Salem.

is a process which not only provides access into mainstreaming schools for the challenged people who have been viewed with disabilities. The manner in which we choose to educate students with disabilities is a consequence of the way we view disabilities.

Need and Significance of the Study

Disabled children need to be educated in Inclusive education programme. Self awareness is able to make changes in the thoughts and interpretations in mind. Changing the interpretations in their mind allows them to change their emotions. Self awareness is one of the attributes of Emotional intelligence and an important factor in achieving success. Interpersonal relationship skills are necessary to uphold them in the group. Interpersonal relationship skills enable them to survive in the normal classroom situation. To achieve a fine rapport with their classmates Interpersonal relationship skills is necessary to uphold them in the group. In Interpersonal skills there are components which are essential to have the better communication, one is listening and another is responding. The above factor leads the investigator to study self awareness and interpersonal relationship skills of visually impaired and hearing impaired.

Statement of the Problem

The problem selected for this study "Self Awareness and Interpersonal Relationship Skills of Disabled Children in Inclusive Education Programme".

Objectives of the Study

1. To study self awareness skills of the disabled children in Inclusive education programme.
2. To study interpersonal relationship skills of the disabled children in Inclusive education programme.

Hypotheses of the Study

1. The disabled children do not differ in their self awareness skill based on their:
   (a) Economic status,
   (b) Type of family,
   (c) Birth order,

2. The disabled children do not differ in their self awareness skill based on their:
   (a) Economic status,
   (b) Type of family,
   (c) Birth order,

Method

Purposive sampling technique was used to gather data from the visually impaired and hearing impaired children. The investigator selected 30 disabled children from inclusive education schools located in Salem district. The investigator developed the self awareness and Interpersonal skills questionnaire. Self awareness skills: The scale consists of 20 statements. Each item provided five responses. The responses were expressed on a five-point scale. Interpersonal relationship skills: The tool consists of 20 statements. Each item provided five responses. The responses were expressed on a five point scale: Every time, Always, Most of time, Sometimes and Never. They weigh 5, 4, 3,2 and 1 for positive statements and 1, 2, 3, 4 and 5 for negative statements.

Analysis of Data and Interpretation

Table 18.1: Shows the Mean Scores of Self Awareness of Disabled Children in Inclusive Education

Variables		N	Mean	SD	't' value		Remark of 0.05 Level
					Calc	Table	
Economic status	<15000	17	62.71	11.75	0.9025	2.58	Not Significant
	>15000	13	67.00	13.78			
Types of family	Nuclear	16	61.94	13.39	0.7563	2.58	Not Significant
	Joint	14	65.47	12.53			
Birth order	First child	11	73.27	7.89	3.6119	2.58	Significant
	Middle child	12	58.55	10.99			
	First child	11	73.27	7.89	4.4903	2.58	Significant
	Last child	7	55.33	7.84			
	Middle child	12	58.55	10.99	0.6159	2.58	Not Significant
	Last child	7	55.33	7.84			

From Table 18.1 it is observed that the disabled child born as first and middle and first and last child differ in their self awareness skills where as the middle and last child do not differ in their self awareness skills. Economic status and types of family have no impact on self awareness skills of these children.

Table 18.2: Shows the Mean Scores of Interpersonal Relationship Skill of Disabled Children in Inclusive Education

Variables		N	Mean	SD	't' value		Remark of 0.05 Level
					Calc	Table	
Economic status	<15000	17	66.71	5.52	2.8277	2.58	Significant
	>15000	13	73.31	7.31			
Types of family	Nuclear	16	68.88	5.99	1.1828	2.58	Not Significant
	Joint	14	71.79	7.49			
Birth order	First child	11	70.09	7.85	0.6072	2.58	Not Significant
	Middle child	12	71.92	6.56			
	First child	11	70.09	7.85	0.9617	2.58	Not Significant
	Last child	7	66.67	4.93			
	Middle child	12	71.92	6.56	1.5025	2.58	Not Significant
	Last child	7	66.67	4.93			

From Table 18.1 it is observed that types of family and birth order of disabled children does not differ in their Interpersonal relationship skills while based on the economics status, the disabled children differ in their Interpersonal relationship skills.

Findings

- The disabled child born as first and middle and first and last child differ in their self awareness skills where as the middle and last child do not differ in their self awareness skills.
- Economic status and types of family have no impact on self awareness skills of these children.
- The types of family and birth order of disabled children does not differ in their Interpersonal relationship skills while based on the economics status, the disabled children differ in their Interpersonal relationship skills.

REFERENCES

Barnitt, V. (2002). *Partial list of Accomplishments and Outcomes Reported by the Florida Inclusion*. Network, Fiscal Year 2001-02.

Deppeleer, Harvey, D., Loreman, T., (2006). Inclusive *Education – A Practical Guide to Supporting Diversity in the Classroom*. Chennai: Allen and Unwin.

Halvorsen, A. T. and Neary, T. (2001). *Building Inclusive Schools: Tools and Strategies for Success*. Needham Heights, MA: Allyn and Bacon.

Mangal, S. K. (2007). Educating *Exceptional Children an Introduction to Special Education*. New Delhi: Prentice-Hall.

Pestonjee, D. M. (1993). *Second Handbook of Psychological and Social Instruments*. New Delhi: Concept Publishing.

Ramesh, G., Ramesh, M., (2010). *The Ace of Soft Skills: Attitude, Communication and Etiquette for Success*. India: Dorling Kindersley.

Ritter, C. L., Michel, C. S., and Irby, B. (1999). *Concerning Inclusion: Perceptions of Middle School Students, their Parents, and Teachers. Rural Special Education Quarterly*, 18(2), 10-17.

Page 125-131

Recent Trend in Educational Research
Edited by: **Dr. D. Sivakumar**
Edition: **2015**
ISBN: 978-93-5056-741-8
Published by: **Discovery Publishing House Pvt. Ltd., New Delhi (India)**

19

Attitude towards Implementing E-Governance in Schools among Headmasters in Kanyakumari District

S. A. Deva Prince

INTRODUCTION

E-Governance is intrinsically linked with the development of computer technology, networking of computers and communication systems. In developing countries, such technologies and systems became available with a perceptible time lag as compared to developed nations. However, in the case of India, with the liberalization of the economy from the early 1990s onwards, there has been a convergence in the availability of cutting edge technologies and opportunities in the field of e-Governance. These innovative methods are to be adopted in the educational management for curricular transaction process, administrative process, etc., so as to uplift the overall performance level of the educational institutions. E-Governance is a novel process that can create remarkable changes in the field of education, thereby become the cause for the development of the nation.

Assistant Professor, Annai Velankanni College, Tholayavattam, K.K. District.

Need and Significance of the Study

ICT offers an opportunity for improvement in public service delivery and most administrative best practices build upon the process redesign and convergence that ICT facilitates. ICT leads to a transformation in work processes and service delivery, lowers transaction cost with improvement in transparency and accountability. It enables transformational change rather than merely technical change. The innovative methods are to be adopted in the educational management for curricular transaction process, administrative process, etc., so as to uplift the overall performance level of the educational institutions. E-Governance is a novel process that can create remarkable changes in the field of education, thereby become the cause for the development of the nation. Considering these factors, the present study was designed and analysed.

E-Governance

According to UNESCO (2002), *'E-Governance'* is "the public sector's use of information and communication technologies with the aim of improving information and service delivery, encouraging citizen participation in the decision-making process and making government more accountable, transparent and effective".

In the present study, it refers to the public sector's use of information and communication technologies with the aim of improving information and service delivery, encouraging citizen participation in the decision-making process and making the school system more accountable, transparent and effective.

Objectives of the Study

To find whether there is any significant difference in the attitude among Headmasters towards implementing e-governance in schools with respect to:

1. Educational District.
2. Gender.
3. Type of School.

Null Hypotheses

Appropriate null hypotheses were framed by the researcher.

Methodology Adopted

The investigator adopted normative survey method for the present study.

Population

The population of the present study was confined to all the Headmasters of higher secondary schools in Kanyakumari district.

Sample

Random sampling method was adopted for the study. In the present study, responses were collected from 141 higher secondary school Headmasters in Kanyakumari district.

Tools Used

E-Governance Attitude Inventory (EGAI) for School HMs (Developed by the Investigator).

Statistical Techniques used

Arithmetic Mean, Standard Deviation, 't' test, ANOVA, Scheffe Test.

Analysis of Data

Null Hypothesis: 1

There is no significant difference among Headmasters of Nagercoil, Thuckalay and Kuzhithurai educational districts in their attitude towards implementing e-governance in schools.

Table 19.1: Difference among Headmasters of Nagercoil, Thuckalay and Kuzhithurai Educational Districts in their Attitude

Educational District	Sum of Squares	Degrees of Freedom	Mean Square	'F'-value	Remarks
Between Groups	1521.577	2	760.789	5.262	Significant
Within Groups	19950.990	138			
Total	21472.577	140	144.572		

(For 2 and 138 degrees of freedom, the table value of 'F' at 5% level of significance is 3.06)

The calculated F-value (5.262) is greater than the table value of 'F' (3.06) at 5 per cent level of significance. Hence the null hypothesis is *rejected*. Thus, there is significant difference among Headmasters of Nagercoil, Thuckalay and Kuzhithurai educational districts in their attitude towards implementing e-governance in schools.

Post HOC Analysis – Scheffe Test

Table 19.2: Difference among Headmasters of Nagercoil, Thuckalay and Kuzhithurai Educational Districts in their Attitude – Scheffe Test

Educational District (I)	Educational District (J)	Mean Difference (I~J)
Nagercoil	Thuckalay	0.95
	Kuzhithurai	6.63*
Thuckalay	Nagercoil	0.95
	Kuzhithurai	7.58*
Kuzhithurai	Nagercoil	6.63*
	Thuckalay	7.58*

*The mean difference is significant at the 0.05 level

The mean difference value shows that there is significant difference between Headmasters of Nagercoil and Kuzhithurai educational districts in their attitude towards implementing e-governance in schools. Similarly, the mean difference value shows that there is significant difference between Headmasters of Thuckalay and Kuzhithurai educational districts in their attitude towards implementing e-governance in schools.

Null Hypothesis: 2

There is no significant difference between Headmasters and Headmistress in their attitude towards implementing e-governance in schools.

Table 19.3: Difference between Headmasters and Headmistress in their Attitude

Gender	N	Mean	SD	't'-value	Remarks
Male	72	112.71	12.837	1.845	Not Significant
Female	69	108.90	11.670		

(For 139 degrees of freedom, the table value of 't' at 5% level of significance is 1.98)

The calculated t-value (1.845) is lesser than the table value (1.98) at 5 per cent level of significance. Hence the null hypothesis is *accepted*. Thus, there is no significant difference between Headmasters and Headmistress in their attitude towards implementing e-governance in schools.

Null Hypothesis: 3

There is no significant difference among Headmasters of Government, Government aided and self-financing schools in their attitude towards implementing e-governance in schools.

Table 19.4: Difference among Headmasters of Government, Government Aided and Self-financing Schools in their Attitude

Educational District	Sum of Squares	Degrees of Freedom	Mean Square	'F'-value	Remarks
Between Groups	346.942	2	173.471	1.133	Not Significant
Within Groups	21125.626	138			
Total	21472.567	140	153.084		

(For 2 and 138 degrees of freedom, the table value of 'F' at 5% level of significance is 3.06)

The calculated F-value (1.133) is lesser than the table value (3.06) at 5 per cent level of significance. Hence the null hypothesis is *accepted*. Thus, there is no significant difference among Headmasters of Government, Government aided and self-financing schools in their attitude towards implementing e-governance in schools.

Discussion of the Result

Based on the findings obtained using the appropriate statistical techniques, a detailed discussion is conducted on various sub variables and presented under the following headings.

At the end of the survey, it was found that 36.17 per cent (51) of the Headmasters were from higher secondary schools of Nagercoil educational district; 33.33 per cent (47) were from Thuckalay educational district and 30.5 per cent were from Kuzhithurai educational district. The rejection of hypothesis-1 shows that there is significant difference among Headmasters of Nagercoil, Thuckalay and Kuzhithurai educational districts in their attitude towards implementing e-governance in schools. The Headmasters of Kuzhithurai educational district have more attitude towards implementing e-governance in schools rather than that of the Headmasters of Nagercoil and Thuckalay educational districts.

The total sample consisted of 51.06 per cent (72) Head masters and 48.94 per cent (69) Headmistress. The acceptance of hypothesis-2 shows that there is no significant difference between Headmasters and Headmistress in their attitude towards implementing e-governance in schools.

The survey result shows that 31.21 per cent (44) of the Headmasters were from Government schools; 38.5 per cent of them were from Government aided schools and the remaining 30.5 per cent of them were from self-financing schools.

The acceptance of hypothesis-3 reveals that there is no significant difference among Headmasters of Government, Government aided and self-financing schools in their attitude towards implementing e-governance in schools.

Conclusion

The purpose of the present investigation is to study the attitude among Headmasters towards implementing e-governance in schools. In this technology era, there are high level revolutionary changes happening day-by-day, moment-to-moment. Since our attitude determines our altitude, the developing attitude to implement e-governance is the first step to bring e-governance into practice and it is a must to implement e-governance in educational institutions to make ourselves fit to survive in this fast-moving entity. The present study clearly revealed that most of the Headmasters have an average level of attitude towards implementing e-governance in schools. This attitude to implement e-governance, especially in the service sectors, most particularly in the field of education is to be developed and brought into favour.

REFERENCES

Ahuja, Amrish Kumar (2007). *Educational Management, Planning and Finance*. New Delhi: Authors Press.

Dash M. and Dash, Neena (2008). *School Management*. New Delhi: Atlantic Publishers.

Devanathan and Gopalakrishnan (2006). "e-Administration an e-Platform for e-Governance to Introduce Transparency and Accountability in Governments and Organizations".<http://www.allacademic.com/meta/p_mla_apa_research_citation/2/8/1/4/7/p.281478_index.html>

Garret, E. Henry (2004). *Statistics in Psychology and Education*. New Delhi: Paragon International.

Monga, Anil (2008). "E-government in India: Opportunities and Challenges". *JOAAG*, Vol. 3, No. 2, pp. 52-61. <http://www.joaag.com/uploads/5_Monga2EGov3_2_.pdf>

Palanisamy, Ramaraj (2004). "Issues and Challenges in e-governance Planning". *Electronic Government, an International Journal*. Vol. 1, No. 3, pp. 253-272. <http://www.inderscience.com/search/index.php?action=record&rec_id=5551>

Prabhu C. S. R. (2005). *E-Governance*. New Delhi: Prentice Hall of India.

Singh, Amar Jeet and Bhardwaj, Mohini (2009). "E-Governance: Single Portal for Integrated Examination System". 287-293. <http://www.csi-sigegov.org/ emerging_pdf/31_287-293.pdf>

Swamy, Raju Narayana (2010). "Effective E-Governance: Exploring the Single Window System in Kerala". *University News*. Vol.48, No. 29, pp. 1-5.

Usmani B. D. (2007). *School Management*. New Delhi: Himalaya Publishing House.

Page 132-139
Recent Trend in Educational Research
Edited by: **Dr. D. Sivakumar**
Edition: **2015**
ISBN: 978-93-5056-741-8
Published by: **Discovery Publishing House Pvt. Ltd., New Delhi (India)**

20

Modernity of IX Standard Students in Thoothukudi District

R. Thangaselvam

INTRODUCTION

Education works as the potential instrument of modernization. The progress of modernization is closely related to the pace of educational development. The spread of education, the preparation of educated and skilled citizens and training of intelligent promote modernization (Sharma, 2002). Most authors agree that modernization is a set of personal qualities, a prerequisite for economic and socio-political development and these qualities are related to traditional, religious and culture values and their re-interpretation or to secular factors such as industrialization, urbanization and education. Modernity is a very controversial and important aspect of our society. It has sparked killings and miracles in many different cultures. Modernity is the basis for our society of the world today, and changes the shape of history every second.

The Rationale of the Study

Education is the prime mover of development. It opens the door to modernization. In the adolescent stage, the students

Assistant Professor in Bio-Science, SCAD College of Education, Cheranmahadevi.

easily get emotional tension. The adolescent might not be fully conversant with the demands of modernity except perhaps some familiarity with modern trends and fashions, particularly those connected with costumes and conversational modes. In order to derive the maximum benefit from a modern dispensation, they have to make the word best, traditional values and the realized mindset that suits the contemporary situation. Keeping these factors in mind the investigator inclined to do a study to seek the current position of Modernity of IX standard students in Thoothukudi district and her wish concluded in the selection of this particular topic for the present study.

Objectives

1. To find out the level of Modernity and its dimensions of IX standard students in terms of total sample.
2. To find out the level of Modernity and its dimensions of IX standard students in terms of gender, medium of study, type of school and monthly income of the family.

Hypotheses

1. There is no significant difference between Modernity and its dimensions of IX standard students with respect to gender.
2. There is no significant difference between Modernity and its dimensions of IX standard students with respect to medium of study.
3. There is no significant difference among Modernity and its dimensions of IX standard students with respect to type of school.
4. There is no significant association between Modernity and its dimensions of IX standard students with respect to monthly income of the family.

Method for the Study

In the present study, the investigator has adopted normative survey method in view of the objectives of the study and to the investigator has adopted questionnaire for yielding information regarding modernity of IX standard students.

Population for the Study

The population of the present study consists of IX standard students studying in Thoothukudi district.

Sample for the Study

The investigator has used the simple random sampling technique to draw a total sample selected for the present study is 500 IX standard students studying from different schools in Thoothukudi District.

Tools used

The investigator has used Modernity scale developed by Antony Sagaya Ruban (2009) and adopted by the investigator as tools for collecting the data.

Statistics used

The investigator had used mean, standard deviation, 't' test, F test (ANOVA), Co-efficient correlation and Chi-square test to analyse the data.

Analysis of Data

Null Hypothesis: 1

There is no significant difference between Modernity and its dimensions of IX standard students with respect to gender.

Table 20.1: Difference between Modernity and Its Dimensions of IX Standard Students with Respect to Gender

Dimensions	Gender	Mean	S.D	Calculated 't' value	Remark
Family	Male (249)	32.37	3.72	0.358	NS
	Female (251)	32.48	3.68		
Society	Male (249)	22.13	2.96	0.535	NS
	Female (251)	22.00	2.73		
Education	Male (249)	48.30	4.54	0.192	NS
	Female (251)	48.37	3.77		
Science and Technology	Male (249)	41.46	4.58	0.045	NS
	Female (251)	41.44	4.32		
Modernity in total	Male (249)	144.27	11.59	0.036	NS
	Female (251)	144.30	10.63		

(At 5% level of significance, the table value of 't' is 1.96)

It is inferred from Table 20.1 that there is no significant difference between male and female IX standard students in modernity in total and its dimensions of family, society, education and science and technology.

Null Hypothesis: 2

There is no significant difference between Modernity and its dimensions of IX standard students with respect to medium of study.

Table 20.2: Difference between Modernity and Its Dimensions of IX Standard Students with Respect to Medium of Study

Dimensions	Medium	Mean	S.D	Calculated 't' value	Remark
Family	Tamil (452)	32.53	3.70	2.127	S
	English (48)	31.38	3.58		
Society	Tamil (452)	22.17	2.81	1.266	NS
	English (48)	21.52	3.16		
Education	Tamil (452)	48.78	3.77	6.263	S
	English (48)	43.90	5.27		
Science and Technology	Tamil (452)	41.77	4.21	4.366	S
	English (48)	38.25	5.43		
Modernity in total	Tamil (452)	145.21	10.35	4.903	S
	English (48)	135.04	13.99		

(At 5% level of significance, the table value of 't' is 1.96)

It is inferred from Table 20.2 that there is no significant difference between English medium and Tamil medium IX standard students in the dimension society. But there is significant difference between English and Tamil medium IX standard students in modernity in total and its dimensions family, education and science and technology. From the mean value it is inferred that Tamil medium IX standard students (mean =32.53) are better than English medium IX standard students (mean =31.38) in the dimension family.

From the mean value it is inferred that Tamil medium IX standard students (mean =48.78) are better than English medium IX standard students (mean =43.90) in the dimension education. From the mean value it is inferred that Tamil medium IX standard students (mean =41.77) are better than English medium IX standard students (mean =38.25) in the dimension science and technology. From the mean value it is inferred that Tamil medium IX standard students (mean

=145.21) are better than English medium IX standard students (mean =135.04) in modernity in total.

Null Hypothesis: 3

There is no significant difference among Modernity and its dimensions of IX standard students with respect to type of school.

Table 20.3: Difference among IX Standard Students in Modernity and its Dimensions with Respect To Type of School

Dimensions	Source of Variation	Sum of Squares	Degrees of Freedom	Calculated 'F' Value	Remark
Family	Between	79.864	2	2.944	NS
	Within	7106.925	524		
Society	Between	47.018	2	2.925	NS
	Within	4211.657	524		
Education	Between	49.081	2	1.414	NS
	Within	9092.798	524		
Science and Technology	Between	5.852	2	0.148	NS
	Within	10384.759	524		
Modernity in total	Between	259.418	2	1.051	NS
	Within	64695.455	524		

(At 5% level of significance for 2,524 df, the table value of 'F' is 3.01)

It is inferred from Table 20.3 that there is no significant difference among Government, Aided and Self-financed school IX standard students in modernity in total and its dimensions family, society, education and science and technology.

Null Hypothesis: 4

There is no significant association between Modernity and its dimensions of XI standard students with respect of monthly income of the family.

It is inferred from Table 20.4 that there is no significant association between monthly income and Modernity in total and its dimensions of family, society, and science and technology of XI standard students. But there is significant association between monthly income and the dimension education of XI standard students.

Table 20.4: Association between Modernity and its Dimensions of IX Standard Students with Respect to Monthly Income of the Family

Dimensions	Degrees of Freedom	Calculated 'χ^2' Value	Remark
Family	4	5.116	NS
Society		6.728	NS
Education		15.260	S
Science and Technology		5.021	NS
Modernity in total		7.564	NS

(For 4 df, at 5% level of significance, the table value of 'χ^2' is 9.488)

Interpretations

1. 't' test result reveals that there is significant difference between English and Tamil medium IX standard students in their attitude towards modernity in total and its dimensions family, education and science and technology. From the mean value it is inferred that Tamil medium IX standard students (mean =32.53) are better than English medium IX standard students (mean =31.38) in their attitude towards the dimension family. From the mean value it is inferred that Tamil medium IX standard students (mean =48.78) are better than English medium IX standard students (mean =43.90) in their attitude towards the dimension education. From the mean value it is inferred that Tamil medium IX standard students (mean =41.77) are better than English medium IX standard students (mean =38.25) in their attitude towards the dimension science and technology. From the mean value it is inferred that Tamil medium IX standard students (mean =145.21) are better than English medium IX standard students (mean =135.04) in their attitude towards modernity in total.

This may due to the fact that Tamil medium students are learning in their mother tongue. Thus it is an advantage for developing their modernity. This makes the students being realistic to the realities around them. The learning in mother tongue facilitates easy understanding and retention of the concept. Thus they are able to express their views in a better manner in their first language. This may be the reason for the high modernity of Tamil medium IX standard students.

2. The chi-square test result reveals that there is significant association between monthly income and in their attitude towards education of IX standard students.

This may due to the fact that the parents with high salary can meet the needs of their children educational and extra-curricular activities. Parents wish that their children should live better than themselves and so they want to provide better opportunities. Parent's income decides life style of the students and provides better exposure and improvement.

Recommendations

1. In order to increase the level of Science and Technology knowledge of the students 'Techno-Modern Scientific Education' can be included as a separate paper.
2. A special curriculum may be framed in such a way that they are updated and help the students to develop the modernity of the students.
3. In order to increase the performance of the students in their modernity, web-based work can be given to them.
4. Co-curricular activities like dancing, photography, music, drawing and painting should be given importance in the curriculum, so that the students can develop their talents.
5. School should organize personality development programmes in order to enhance the level of modernity.

Conclusion

The present investigation points out positive result of Modernity and its dimensions. The study may find some usefulness in the field of modern education and may serve as database for future research. This knowledge would be of immense important to the teacher educators, educational planners and society at large.

REFERENCES

Aggarwal, J. C. (1966), *Educational Research: An Introduction*, Arya Book Depot, New Delhi.

Aggarwal, J.C. (1995), *Teacher and Education in Developing Society*, Vikas Publishing House Pvt. Ltd., New Delhi.

Aggarwal, Y. P. (1990), *Statistical Methods, Concepts, Applications and Computations*, Sterling Publishers Pvt. Ltd., New Delhi.

Aiyar, S. P. (1973), *Modernization of Traditional Society*, Mac Millan, India.

Antony Sahaya Ruban and Annaraja (2009), Relationship between Modernity and Temperament of Higher Secondary Students, Unpublished M.Phil Dissertation, St. Xavier's College of Education, Palayamkottai.

Atlas, S. H. (1970), *Modernization and Social Change*, Angus and Robertson Publishers, Sydney.

Best, W. John (1986), *Research in Education*, Prentice Hall of India Pvt. Ltd., New Delhi.

Best, W. John and Kahn, V. James (1992), *Research in Education 7th edition*, Prentice Hall of India Pvt. Ltd., New Delhi.

Bhatnagar, S (2001), *Advanced Educational Psychology*, Surya Publication, Meerut.

Kothari, C.R. (1990), *Research Methodology* – Methods and Techniques, Wishwa Prakashan, New Delhi.

Walter, R. Borg and Gall, Meredith Damien (1979), *Educational Research*, Longman, New York.

Page 140-149
Recent Trend in Educational Research
Edited by: **Dr. D. Sivakumar**
Edition: **2015**
ISBN: 978-93-5056-741-8
Published by: **Discovery Publishing House Pvt. Ltd., New Delhi (India)**

21

Influence of Multiple Intelligence and Achievement of Secondary Teacher Education Students

Dr. K. Rajasekaran

INTRODUCTION

Howard Gardner of Harvard has identified seven distinct intelligences. This theory has emerged from recent cognitive research and "documents the extent to which students possess different kinds of minds and therefore learn, remember, perform, and understand in different ways," according to Gardner (1991). According to this theory, "we are all able to know the world through language, logical-mathematical analysis, spatial representation, musical thinking, the use of the body to solve problems or to make things, an under standing of other individuals, and an understanding of ourselves. Where individuals differ is in the strength of these intelligences – the so-called profile of intelligences – and in the ways in which such intelligences are invoked and combined to carry out different tasks, solve diverse problems, and progress in various domains." Gardner says that these differences "challenge an educational system that assumes that everyone can learn the same materials in the same way and

Principal, C.K. College of Education, Cuddalore.

that a uniform, universal measure suffices to test student learning. Indeed, as currently constituted, our educational system is heavily biased toward linguistic modes of instruction and assessment and, to a somewhat lesser degree, toward logical-quantitative modes as well." Gardner argues that "a contrasting set of assumptions is more likely to be educationally effective. Students learn in ways that are identifiably distinctive.

Multiple Intelligence

Gardner proposes eight different intelligences to account for a broader range of human potential in children and adults. These intelligences are:

- *Verbal-Linguistic Intelligence:* well-developed verbal skills and sensitivity to the sounds, meanings and rhythms of words.
- *Mathematical-Logical Intelligence*: ability to think conceptually and abstractly, and capacity to discern logical or numerical patterns.
- *Musical Intelligence*: ability to produce and appreciate rhythm, pitch and Timber.
- *Visual-Spatial Intelligence:* capacity to think in images and pictures, to visualize accurately and abstractly.
- *Bodily-Kinesthetic Intelligence*: ability to control one's body movements and to handle objects skillfully.
- *Interpersonal Intelligence*: capacity to detect and respond appropriately to The moods, motivations and desires of others.
- *Intrapersonal Intelligence*: capacity to be self-aware and in tune with inner feelings, values, beliefs and thinking processes.
- *Naturalist Intelligence*: ability to recognize and categorize plants, animals and other objects in nature.
- *Existential Intelligence*: sensitivity and capacity to tackle deep questions about human existence, such as the meaning of life, why do we die, and how did we get here.

Need for the Study

All students can learn and succeed but not all on the same day in the same way. Intelligence in the ability to see a problem, then solve a problem or make something that is useful to a group of people. Howard Gardner's theory of Multiple Intelligence identifies that there are many forms of intelligence and that people have varying strengths and combination of these. We can all improve each of the intelligence area then in others. With an understanding of Gardner's theory of Multiple Intelligence, teachers, school administrators and parents can better understand the learners in their midst. They can allow the students to safely explore and learn in many ways and they can help students direct their own learning. Teachers can help students understand and appreciate their strengths, and identify the real-world activities that will stimulate more learning.

Today in this world, technological advancement and Multiple Intelligence plays a vital role. Application of Multiple Intelligence theory helps students begin to understand how they are intelligent. The theory of multiple intelligences also has strong implications for adult learning and development. Many adults find themselves in jobs that do not make optimal use of their most highly developed intelligences. The theory of multiple intelligences gives adults a whole new way to look at their lives; examining potentials that they left behind in their childhood but now have the opportunity to develop through courses, hobbies, or other programmes of self-development.

In this context, the prospective teachers are in the need of utilizing their intelligence to the maximum extent for becoming as an effective teacher in the future. Hence it is the responsibility of the teacher educators to provide a greater platform to utilize the optimum level of multiple intelligence of in-service teacher. The researchers are warranted to know the influence of multiple intelligence among in-service and pre-service teacher in the present context. Thus it was thought prudential by the investigator to select influence of Multiple Intelligence and achievement of prospective teachers.

Statement of the Problem

The problem entitle on "Influence of Multiple Intelligence and Achievement of Secondary Teacher Education Students'.

By the term 'Multiple Intelligence' the investigator means a set of skills such as Verbal-linguistic intelligence, Logical-mathematical intelligence, Visual-spatial intelligence, Bodily-kinesthetic intelligence, Musical-rhythmic intelligence, Interpersonal intelligence and Intrapersonal intelligence.

Objectives

1. To find out the level of multiple intelligence of secondary teacher education students.
2. To find out the significant difference if any on multiple intelligence of secondary teacher education students in terms of certain selected demographic variables.
3. To find out the relationship if any among multiple intelligences of secondary teacher education students.
4. To find out the relationship if any between multiple intelligence and academic achievements of secondary teacher education students.

Hypotheses

1. There is a significant difference exist if any on multiple intelligence of secondary teacher education students in terms of certain selected demographic variables such as gender, locality and subject study.
2. There is a significant relation among multiple intelligences of secondary teacher education students.
3. There is a significant relation between multiple intelligence and academic achievements of secondary teacher education students.

Methodology

The investigator has adopted the descriptive survey method of research to study the Multiple Intelligence of prospective teachers. Survey research is a procedure in which information is systematically collected from a population through some form of questionnaire or schedule.

Tools

- *Multiple Intelligence Inventory: 'Multiple Intelligence Inventory'* developed by Armstrong (1993) is taken as base tool for this investigation to assess the multiple intelligence of the prospective teachers. Further it was modified by the investigator with consultation of guide and experts with reliability and validity. The statements of multiple intelligence are given with five point rating scale such as strongly agree, agree, undecided, disagree and strongly disagree with 5, 4, 3, 2, 1 scores for the positive statements and the negative statements are scored reversely. The reliability of the multiple intelligence inventory is 0.825 is established by using Kuder-Richardson method.

- *Academic Achievement:* The marks of all subjects in their model exams conducted by the college as recorded in the respective college were taken as the achievement score of the secondary teacher education students.
- *Locale and Sample:* The secondary teacher education means those who are studying currently in the college of education in graduation under Tamilnadu teachers education university is the population of this study. The investigator taken as sample of 150 secondary teacher education students from cuddalore district for the present investigation.

Findings

It is found that 17.6 per cent of the boys have low, 69.6 per cent average and 12.8 per cent high levels of multiple intelligence. Among the girls 20.0 per cent of students have low, 66.0 per cent average and 14.0 per cent high levels of multiple intelligence.

It is inferred from Table 21.1 that 16 per cent of the boys have low, 62.4 per cent average and 21.60 per cent high levels of achievement. Among the girls 14.67 per cent of students have low, 64 per cent average and 21.33 per cent high levels of achievement.

It is found that there is no significance on multiple intelligence between Male and Female prospective teachers at 0.01 level. Hence the formulated hypothesis is rejected. Therefore Men and Women are not difference in their multiple intelligence. It is observed that there is significance difference on multiple intelligence of B.Ed. students in terms of their Rural and Urban residency at 0.01 level. Hence the formulated

Table 21.1: Significance Difference on Multiple Intelligence of Secondary Teacher Education Students in Relation to Gender, Locale and Subjects Studied

Category		Mean	SD	N	Calculated value 't'	Remarks
Gender	Male	77.82	16.73	070	0.69	Not Significant 5% level of significance
	Female	75.41	15.21	080		
Locale	Rural	65.12	15.53	110	3.20	Significant 1% level of significance
	Urban	72.41	16.21	040		
Subjects studied	Language	68.32	15.36	030	3.56	Significant 1% level of significance
	Arts/Social science	72.57	16.46	030		
	Science	77.28	16.89	090		

hypothesis is accepted. It is formed that prospective teachers from urban residency are having more multiple intelligence (72.41) than the rural (65.12) based secondary teacher education students..

In consideration of subjects studied by the secondary teacher education students. There exist significance difference on multiple intelligence of prospective teachers in terms of their subjects studied at 0.01 level. Hence the formulated hypothesis is accepted. It is found that science B.Ed trainees (77.28) are having higher multiple intelligence followed by arts for social science teachers (72.57) and language (68.32) B.Ed trainees.

It is observed that there exist a significant positive low correlation exist among multiple intelligence of B.Ed trainees 0.01 level. Hence the formulated hypothesis is accepted. It is found that there is positive low correlation between: verbal linguistic and mathematical logical (0.235), verbal linguistic and musical (0.158), verbal linguistic and visual – spatial (0.358), verbal and bodily – kinesthetic (0.127), verbal linguistic and interpersonal (0.278), verbal linguistic and intrapersonal (0.486): mathematical logical and musical (0.385), mathematical logical and visual – spatial (0.362), mathematical logical and bodily – kinesthetic (0.266), mathematical logical and interpersonal (0.217), mathematical logical and intrapersonal (0.209):

Table 21.2: Significance Correlation among Multiple Intelligence of Secondary Teacher Education Students

M.I	Verbal-Linguistic	Mathematical Logical	Musical	Visual-Spatial	Bodily-Kinesthetic	Inter-personal	Intra-personal
Verbal-Linguistic	1.00	0.235	0.158	0.358	0.127	0.278	0.486
Mathe-matical Logical		1.00	0.385	0.362	0.266	0.217	0.209
Musical			1.00	0.256	0.387	0.487	0.384
Visual-Spatial				1.00	0.211	0.384	0.447
Bodily-Kines-thetic					1.00	0.452	0.339
Inter-personal						1.00	0.428
Intra-personal							**1.00**

'r' value Significant at 0.01 level

musical and visual – spatial (0.256), musical and bodily – kinesthetic (0.387), musical and intrapersonal (0.487), musical and intrapersonal (0.384): visual – spatial and bodily – kinesthetic (0.211), visual – spatial and intrapersonal (0.384), visual – spatial and intrapersonal (0.447): bodily – kinesthetic and interpersonal (0.452), bodily – kinesthetic and intrapersonal (0.339), interpersonal and intrapersonal (0.428). (Table 21.2)

Table 21.3: Significance Correlation between Multiple Intelligence and Academic Achievement of Secondary Teacher Education Students

	Language	Arts/Social Science	Science
Multiple Intelligence	0.386	0.568	0.785

'r' value Significant at 0.01 level

1. There exist significance correlation between multiple intelligence and academic achievement of secondary

teacher education students in language, arts for social science and science at 0.01 level hence the formulated hypothesis is accepted. It is found that there is positive low correlation between multiple intelligence and language secondary teacher education students (0.386). It is also found that there is high positive correlation between multiple intelligence and arts and social science (0.568) and multiple intelligence and science (0.785) B.Ed trainees.

Summary on Findings

From the present study it is concluded that multiple intelligence have influence on native of residency and subject studied prospective teachers and not made any significance difference regarding Gender of the prospective teachers. Further it is clearly known that urban prospective teachers are exceed on multiple intelligence than rural. Likewise science prospective teachers are better multiple intelligence than the arts for social science and language teachers respectively. It is clearly evident that there is positive correlation among multiple intelligence of perspective teachers and also with academic achievement of prospective teachers.

Implications and Conclusion

Based on the findings study recommended that urban prospective teachers has to be given more attention to increase their multiple intelligence in the in service programme, and also language and arts for social science prospective teachers will be focusing more on multiple intelligence training in future.

Further the development of multiple intelligence will need to the academic achievement of the prospective teachers. Hence the curriculum said as and policy-makes should incorporate the development of multiple intelligence in the curriculam.

Conclusion

Each student has an individual profile of characteristics, abilities and challenges that result from learning and development. These manifest as individual differences in intelligence, creativity, cognitive style, motivation and the capacity to process information, communicate and relate to others. Two fundamental assumptions that underlie formal education systems are: *(a)* students retain knowledge and skills they acquire in classroom; and *(b)* they can apply them in situations outside the classroom. But are these assumptions accurate? Students who are high in creative intelligence are often not on the top rank of their class. The reason behind is that instead of giving conformist answers, they give unique answers, for which they get marked down. Likewise, students with high practical intelligence often do not relate well to the demands of school. However, these students often do well outside the classroom. They might have excellent social skills and good common sense. Therefore, students should be given opportunities to learn through creative and practical thinking, in addition to conventional strategies that focus on simply 'learning' and remembering a body of information. It is important in teaching to balance instruction related to different types of intelligence. Teachers could develop multiple intelligences in the classroom step-wise, that is, identify instructional goals and objectives; consider activities that may help the students in the development of multiple intelligences; limit the number of activities to two or three; consider what resources and materials he will need to implement the lesson; specify a time-frame for the lesson; provide an opportunity for reflection by students; and integrate assessment into the learning process.

REFERENCES

Ajithraj. N.D and Sebastian. S (2005). A Study on Learning Styles and Multiple Intelligence of B.Ed. Student, Unpublished M.Phil thesis, M.S University, Tirunelveli, Tamil Nadu.

Anisha V. Gopalakrishnan (2007). Relationship between Multiple Intelligence and Knowledge of Content Pedagogy of Natural Science of Secondary Teacher Education Students. *Stella Mautine Journal of Education Research.* Vol. 1, No. 2.

Annaraja. P and Anthony Muthu. P. (2009). A Study on Multiple Intelligence of Primary School Teachers, Unpublished M.Phill thesis, Tamil Nadu Teachers Education University, Chennai, Tamil Nadu.

Antony Gracious, F.L. and Annaraja, P. (2011). Multiple Intelligence and Computer Efficacy of Prospective Teachers. *Meston Journal of Research in Education,* Vol.10, No. 1.

Baer and Jeffrey Scott (2010). The Relationship of Multiple Intelligence Instruction to Sight Singing Achievement of Middle School Choral Students. Vol. 71, No. 04.

Basic Book

Degennaro and Alfred, J. (2010). Application of Multiple Intelligence Theory to an E-learning Technology Acceptance Model. Vol. 71, No. 06.

Gardener, H. (1993). Multiple Intelligences: The Theory in Practice. New York: Basic Books.

Gardner, H. (1999). Intelligences Reframed: Multiple Intelligences for the 21st Century. New York. Basic Books.

Gardner, Howard. (1983). *Frames of Mind: The Theory of Multiple Intelligences.* New York:

Gardner, Howard. (2000). *Intelligence Reframed: Multiple Intelligences for the 21st Century.*

Gowen and Deborah, C. (2010). The Relationship of Motivation and Multiple Intelligence Preference to Achievement from Instruction using Webquests. ProQuest LLC, Ed.D. Dissertation, Walden University Doctoral Dissertations.

Hema Nalini (2008). A Study on Impact of the Theory of Multiple Intelligence on Children with Autism. New Frontiers in Education. Vol. 41, No. 4.

Mangal, S. K. (2008). Essentials of Educational Psychology. Printice Hall of India Private Limited, New Delhi.

Ozgen, Kemal, Tataroglu, Berna, Alkan and Huseyin (2011). An Examination of Multiple Intelligence Domains and Learning Styles of Pre-service Mathematics Teachers; Their Reflection on Mathematics Education. *Educational Research and Reviews,* Vol. 6 No. 2 pp. 168-181, Feb 2011.

Page 150-162

Recent Trend in Educational Research
Edited by: **Dr. D. Sivakumar**
Edition: **2015**
ISBN: 978-93-5056-741-8
Published by: **Discovery Publishing House Pvt. Ltd., New Delhi (India)**

22

A Study on Learning Styles and Academic Achievement in Social Science of High School Students

J. Murali

INTRODUCTION

Learning styles are simply put, various approaches or ways of learning. They involve educating methods, particular to an individual that are presumed to allow that individual to learn best. It is commonly believed that most people favor some particular method of interacting with, taking in, and processing stimuli or information. Based on this concept, the idea of individualized 'learning styles' originated in the 1970s, and has gained popularity in recent years. It has been proposed that teachers should assess the learning styles of their students and adapt their classroom methods to best fit each student's learning style. Learning style is an important factor in the academic achievement of the students. Some students have good learning styles, some students may have poor learning styles which may be due to several factors such as family background, economic status, size of the family, education of the parents etc. Individual differences also play a vital role in learning styles of children.

Assistant Professor, Paulsons Teacher Training College, Pullichapallam, Villupuram.

Learning styles may be different from child to child and they also differ in case of high, average and low achiever. And the learning styles also vary among the students from school to school, management to management, locality to locality, etc.

In our present societal setup, school serves as one major instrument in imparting knowledge. It has become mandatory and obligation for the parents and the government to provide education to all children in our nation. In this scenario, no child is entitled to lose the privilege of studying in a school. All school entrants, from beginning to end, require some styles and practice them to successfully pursue knowledge. These achieved test score determines their future career. The ambitions and aspirations of our students are largely governed by their learning skills adopted by the students. Kothari Commission states, at the outset, the destiny of a nation is shaped in classrooms. If such a weightage is given to students, how much more weightage should be given to their academic and learning styles. The investigator is brimmed with the zest to know whether there is any relationship between learning styles and academic achievement in social science of high school students.

Statement of the Problem

The present study is entitled as 'A Study on Learning Styles and Academic Achievement in Social Science of High School Students'.

Operational Key term Definition

Learning Styles

Learning styles refer to the different ways of learning; the seven specific types of learning styles developed by various psychologists are: linguistic, logical, spatial, musical, bodily, interpersonal and intrapersonal.

Academic Achievement in Social Science

Academic achievement is nothing but educational attainment, which refers to the gains, got by the pupils as a result of education. Verbal and numerical ability of an individual is referred to as one's academic achievement. Here, the investigator means the attainment got in Social Science. No separate tool was prepared by the investigator to measure the achievement score in Social science. The marks in social science subjects in their half yearly exams conducted by the school as recorded in the respective school register were taken as the achievement score in social science.

Objectives

1. To find out the level of learning styles and its dimensions such as: visual, auditory and kinesthetic of high school students.
2. To find out the level of learning styles and its dimensions such as visual, auditory and kinesthetic of high school students with reference to gender.
3. To find out whether there is any significant difference between male and female high school students in learning styles and its dimensions.
4. To find out whether there is any significant difference between rural and urban school students in learning styles and its dimensions.
5. To find out whether there is any significant difference among government, aided and unaided high school students in learning styles and its dimensions.
6. To find out whether there is any significant relationship between learning styles and academic achievement in social science of high school students.

Hypotheses

1. The level of learning styles and its dimensions such as visual, auditory and kinesthetic of high school students is average.
2. The level of learning styles and its dimensions such as visual, auditory and kinesthetic of high school students with reference to gender is average.
3. There is no significant difference between male and female high school students in learning styles and its dimensions.
4. There is no significant difference between rural and urban students in learning styles and its dimensions.
5. There is no significant difference among government, aided and unaided high school students in learning styles and its dimensions.

6. There is no significant relationship between learning styles and academic achievement in social science of high school students.

Method of the Study

Research methods are of utmost important in a research process. A pre-planned and well-described method will provide the researcher a scientific and feasible plan for attacking and solving the problem under investigation. The investigator has adopted survey method in view of the objectives of the study.

Population and Sample

"A population is any group of individual objects that have one or more characteristics in common that are of interests to the research" (Sidhy, 1984, p. 253). The population of the present study consists of high school, IXth standard students studying in Villupuram District. A sample is a small portion of the population selected for observation and analysis. The investigator took a sample of 300 students for his study.

Tools

The tool prepared and developed by Victoria Chislett and Alan Chapman (2005) the tool under 30 statements. Each item contains three options such as Visual, Auditory and Kinaesthetic. Hence, each respondent could fall under any one of the above options. There is no right or wrong answer for each of the 30 statements.

Scoring

The learning styles inventory consists of 30 objective type questions. There is no right or wrong answers to these questions. Each answer mentions different learning styles. Students' selection of the 1st, 2nd, 3rd, options for item indicates *(i)* Visual, *(ii)*. Auditory, *(iii)*. Kinaesthetic correspondingly and the scoring/the mark allotment is 1.

Establishing Validity And Reliability

Content Validity

The tool is standardized but the investigator established validity for our location of the present environment. The tool was given to some experts in the field and his guide for their opinions and comments for establishing content validity.

Reliability

Reliability is the degree of accuracy and consistency. The prepared tool was subjected to test-retest method. Again the same tool was administered to the same set of students after an interval of a week. The responses of the respondents were scored and the correlation co-efficient was found to be 0.84 for the two sets of scores. Thus the reliability of the tool was established.

1. The level of learning styles and its dimensions such as visual, auditory and kinesthetic of high school students is average.

Table 22.1: Level of Learning Styles of High School Students

Sl. No.	Dimensions	Low		Average		High	
		Count	%	Count	%	Count	%
1.	Visual	56	18.7	200	66.7	44	14.7
2.	Auditory	70	23.3	181	60.3	49	16.3
3.	Kinesthetic	70	23.3	173	57.7	57	19.0
4.	Learning Styles	73	24.3	173	57.7	54	18.0

From Table 22.1 it is inferred that the level of learning styles and its dimensions such as visual, auditory and kinesthetic of high school students is average.

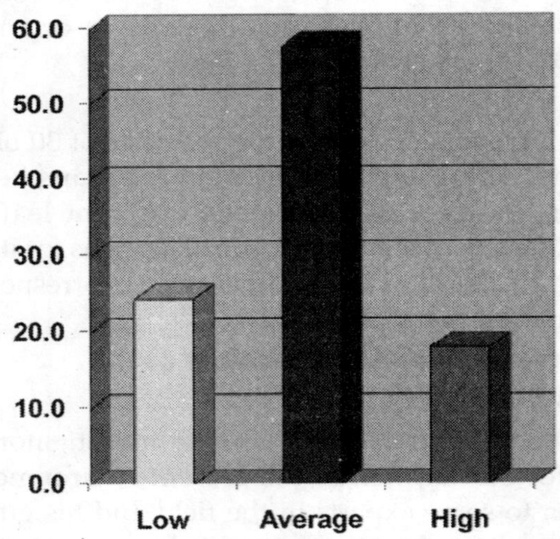

Fig. 22.1: Level of Learning Styles of High School Students

2. The level of learning styles and its dimensions such as: visual, auditory and kinesthetic of high school students with reference to gender is average.

Table 22.2: Level of Learning Styles of Boys and Girls High School Students

Sl. No.	Dimensions	Gender	Low		Average		High	
			Count	%	Count	%	Count	%
1.	Visual	Male	32	23.2	91	65.9	15	10.9
		Female	24	14.8	109	67.3	29	17.9
2.	Auditory	Male	40	29.0	83	60.1	15	10.9
		Female	30	18.5	98	60.5	34	21.0
3.	Kinesthetic	Male	35	25.4	90	65.2	13	9.4
		Female	30	18.5	103	63.6	29	17.9
4.	Learning Styles	Male	44	31.9	69	50.0	25	18.1
		Female	29	17.9	104	64.2	29	17.9

From Table 22.2 it is inferred that the level of learning styles and its dimensions such as: visual, auditory and kinesthetic of boys and girls student is average.

3. There is no significant difference between male and female high school students in learning styles and its dimensions.

Table 22.3: Difference between Male and Female Students in Learning Styles

Dimensions	Gender	Mean	SD	N	Calculated 't' value	Table Value at 5% Level	Remark
Visual	Male	27.61	9.03	138	2.81	1.96	S
	Female	30.56	9.14	162			
Auditory	Male	24.38	8.46	138	2.72	1.96	S
	Female	27.07	8.59	162			
Kinesthetic	Male	30.25	8.89	138	2.77	1.96	S
	Female	33.12	8.98	162			
Learning Styles	Male	156.72	47.63	138	3.07	1.96	S
	Female	172.65	41.17	162			

Since the calculated value of 't' is higher than the table value at 5 per cent level of significance, there is significant difference between male and female high school students in learning styles and its dimensions.

4. There is no significant difference between rural and urban students in learning styles and its dimensions.

Table 22.4: Difference between Rural and Urban Students in Learning Styles

Dimensions	Nativity of the Learner	Mean	SD	N	Calculated 't' value	Table Value at 5% Level	Remark
Visual	Rural	25.61	9.43	147	7.14	1.96	S
	Urban	32.65	7.52	153			
Auditory	Rural	18.29	4.34	147	28.79	1.96	S
	Urban	33.08	4.56	153			
Kinesthetic	Rural	28.23	9.27	147	7.23	1.96	S
	Urban	35.24	7.35	153			
Learning Styles	Rural	137.11	37.83	147	13.47	1.96	S
	Urban	192.43	33.01	153			

Since the calculated value of 't' is higher than the table value at 5 per cent level of significance, there is significant difference between rural and urban students in learning styles and its dimensions.

5. There is no significant difference among government, aided and unaided high school students in learning styles and its dimensions.

Table 22.5: Difference among Government, Aided and Unaided School Students in Learning Styles

Dimensions	Source	Sum of Squares	Degrees of Freedom	Mean Square Value	Calculated Value	Remarks at 5% Level
Visual	Between	30482.31	2	10241.16	615.18	Significant
	Within	4944.28	297	16.65		
Auditory	Between	8268.00	2	4134.00	87.04	Significant
	Within	14105.67	297	47.49		
Kinesthetic	Between	19565.44	2	9782.72	579.24	Significant
	Within	5015.97	297	16.89		
Learning Styles	Between	466372.00	2	233186.00	494.23	Significant
	Within	140131.00	297	471.82		

[For 2, 297 degrees of freedom at 5 % level of significance, the table value 'F' is 3.03]

It is inferred from Table 22.5 that there is significant difference among government, aided and unaided high school students in learning styles and its dimensions.

6. The level of academic achievement in social science of high school students is average.

Table 22.6: Level of Academic Achievement in Social Science High School Students

Dimensions	Low		Average		High	
	Count	%	Count	%	Count	%
Academic Achievement	77	25.7	174	58.0	49	16.3

It is inferred from Table 22.6 that 25.7 per cent of the higher secondary students have low, 58.0 per cent of them have average level and 16.3 per cent of them have high level of academic achievement in social science.

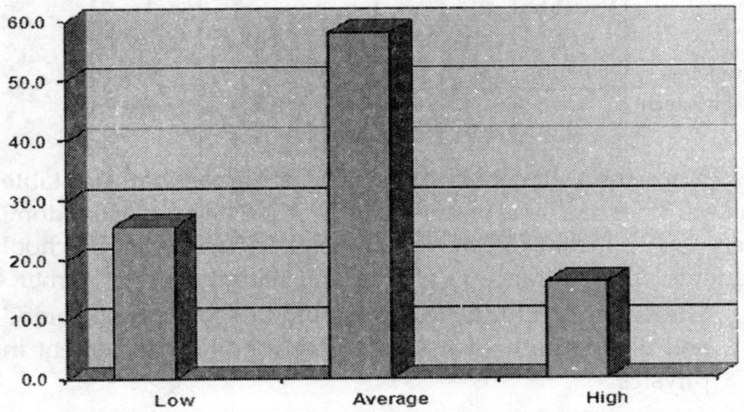

Fig. 22.2: Level of Academic Achievement in Social Science of High School Students

7. The level of academic achievement in social science of boys and girls student is average.

Table 22.7: Level of Academic Achievement of Boys and Girls Students

Variable	Gender	Low		Average		High	
		Count	%	Count	%	Count	%
Academic	Male	43	31.2	79	57.2	16	11.6
Achievement	Female	34	21.0	95	58.6	33	20.4

It is inferred from Table 22.7 that 31.2 per cent of the male students have low, 57.2 per cent of them have average level and 11.6 per cent of them have high level of academic achievement in Social science. Regarding female students, 21.0 per cent of them have low, 58.6 per cent of them have average level and 20.4 per cent of them have high level of academic achievement in social science.

8. There is no significant difference in academic achievement in social science of high school students with reference to Gender and Nativity of the learner.

Table 22.8: Difference in Academic Achievement in Social Science of High School Students with Reference to Gender and Nativity of the Learner

Variables	Back-ground Variables	Mean	SD	N	Calculated 't' value	Table Value at 5% Level	Remark
Academic Achievement	Male	66.56	17.40	138	3.01	1.96	S
	Female	72.70	17.83	162			
	Rural	62.81	18.70	147	7.23	1.96	S
	Urban	62.81	18.70	147			

Since the calculated value of 't' is higher than the table value at 5 per cent level of significance for 298 degrees of freedom, there is significant difference in social science of high school students with reference to gender and nativity of the learner.

9. There is no significant difference among government, aided and unaided school students in academic achievement in physics.

Table 22.9: Difference among Government, Aided and Unaided School Students in Academic Achievement in Social Science

Variable	Source	Sum of Squares	Degrees of Freedom	Mean Square Value	Calculated value	Remarks at 5% Level
Academic Achievement	Between	83783.35	2	41891.63	1010.93	Significant
	Within	12307.25	297	41.440		

[For 2, 297 degrees of freedom at 5 % level of significance, the table value 'F' is 3.03]

Since the calculated value of 'F' is greater than table, it is inferred from Table 22.9 that the hypothesis is rejected. That is, there is significant difference among government, aided and unaided school students in academic achievement in social science.

10. There is no significant relationship between learning styles and academic achievement in social science of high school students.

Table 22.10: Relationship between Learning Styles and Academic Achievement in Social Science

N	Calculated Value of 'Υ'	Table Value of 'Υ'	Remarks at 5% Level
300	0.928	0.113	S

Since the calculated value of '¡' is greater than the table value for 298 degrees of freedom at 5 per cent level of significance, the hypothesis is rejected. That is, there is significant relationship between learning styles and academic achievement in social science of high school students.

Findings

- The level of learning styles and its dimensions such as visual, auditory and kinesthetic of high school students is average.
- The level of learning styles and its dimensions such as visual, auditory and kinesthetic of high school students with reference to gender is average. Among the average value female learning style score is high 64.2 per cent and Male learning style score is low 50 per cent.
- There is significant difference between male and female high school students in learning styles and its dimensions.
- There is significant difference between rural and urban school students in learning styles and its dimensions.
- There is significant difference among government, aided and unaided high school students in learning styles and its dimensions.

- The level of academic achievement in social science of high school students is average. 58.0 per cent of high school students have average level of academic achievement in social science.
- The level of academic achievement in social science of high school boys and girls is average. 57.2 per cent of male students have average level of academic achievement in social science. 58.6 per cent of female students have average level of academic achievement in social science.
- There is significant difference between male and female higher secondary students in academic achievement in social science.
- There is significant difference between rural and urban school students in Academic Achievement in social science.
- There is significant difference among government, aided and unaided school students in academic achievement in social science.
- There is significant relationship between learning styles and academic achievement in social science of high school students.

Discussion on the Result

The 't' test result reveals that there is significant difference between boys and girls in learning style and its dimension the high school girls are better than the boys. This may be due to the fact that the girls are having a very good memory power and remarkable ability to repeat everything what they have learnt. Girls spend most of the time by watching movies, day dreaming and staying as far away from reality as possible. But they are very good at working with colours and pictures. There is significant difference between rural and urban students in learning style and its dimensions the urban students are better than the rural students. This may be due to the fact that the urban students learn variety of languages at a time and to use them whenever it is necessary. Urban students have more chances to attend problem-solving ability tests by attending seminars etc. And also urban students are not attached more with their peers so as to perform their goodness individually.

The 'F' test result reveals that there is significant difference among government, aided and unaided school students in learning style and its dimension unaided school students are better than government and aided school students. This may be due to the fact that the unaided school students have sufficient number of language laboratories for learning new languages than government and aided school students.

The 't' test result reveals that there is significant difference between male and female high school students in their academic achievement in social science and the female students are better than the male students. This may be due to the fact that the female students are well memorized and they are concentrating more only towards the academic subjects of their curriculum. There is significant difference between rural and urban students in their academic achievement in social science and the urban students are better than the rural students. This may be due to the fact that the urban students have a sufficient exposure for learning the subjects and they may have the provision of internet for browsing in schools and home.

The 'F' test result reveals that there is significant difference among government, aided and unaided school students in their academic achievement in social science and the unaided school students are better than the government and the aided school students. This may be due to the fact that most of the unaided schools follow a very good teaching methodology and the students of these schools are very sincere and serious in their studies. Mainly they are to complete their home-work regularly which will lead them to get better performance in their academic activities.

REFERENCES

Aggarwal, J. C. (2004). History of Modern Indian Education, 5th ed., Vikas Publishing House (P) Ltd., New Delhi.

Aggarwal, Y. P. (1990). Statistical Methods, Concepts, Applications and Computations, Sterling Pvt. Ltd., New Delhi.

Best, John W. (1995). Research in Education, 7th edition, Prentice Hall of India Kahn, James V., Pvt Ltd., M-97, Cannaught Circus, New Delhi - 110 001.

Biswas, A., Aggarwal, J. C. (1988). Education in India, Arya Book Depot, New Delhi.

John W. Best, (1986). Research in Education, Prentice Hall of India Pvt. Ltd., New Delhi.

Kakkar, S. B. (1993). Changing Perspectives in Education, Vikas Publishing House Pvt. Ltd., New Delhi.

Kothari, C. R. (1990). Research Methodology - Methods and Techniques, Wishwa Prakashan, New Delhi.

Lokesh Koul (1999). Methodology of Educational Research, Vikas Publishing House Pvt. Ltd., New Delhi, p. 111.

Macmillan and Schumacher (1984). Research in Education, A conceptual Introduction, Little Brown, Boston, USA.

Choudhry, J. C. (1994). "Research Notes, Pathology of Learning", Indian Educational Review, Vol. 29, No. 3-4, July-Oct. 94.

Page 163-169
Recent Trend in Educational Research
Edited by: **Dr. D. Sivakumar**
Edition: **2015**
ISBN: 978-93-5056-741-8
Published by: **Discovery Publishing House Pvt. Ltd., New Delhi (India)**

23

Emotional Intelligence of Higher Secondary Commerce Students in Tiruchendur Taluk

C. Seenivasan

INTRODUCTION

Education is a continuous and life-long process. It is the process of development from the infancy to maturity. It includes the effect of everything, which influences human personality. Education brings changes in individual's behaviour. Education is an activity or a process, which transforms the behaviour of a person from 'instinctive behaviours' to 'human behaviour'. According to Nunn "Education is the complete development of the individually so that he can make an original contribution to his best capacity" (Rai, B. C., 1991, p. 3).

Emotions are often powerful reactions, so it would seem at first glance that everyone ought to be able to recognize their own feelings. In fact, however, this is not always the case. Some persons are highly aware of their own emotions and their thoughts about them, but others seem to be almost totally obvious to these. What are the implications of such differences? *First*, to the extent individuals are not aware of their own emotions and their thoughts about them, but others

Ph.D. Scholar, Bharatiyar University, Coimbatore.

seem to be almost totally obvious to these. What are the implications of such differences? *First,* to the extent individuals are not aware of their own feelings, they cannot make intelligent choices.

Second, because such persons aren't aware of their own emotions, they are often low in expressiveness – they don't show their feelings clearly through facial expressions, body language, or other cues most of use to recognize others' feelings. This can have adverse effects on their interpersonal relationships, because other people find it hard to know how they arc feeling or reacting. For these reasons, this first component of emotional intelligence seems to be quite important.

Emotional intelligence can be developed by improving emotional competencies paving the way for making life more healthy, enjoyable and successful. In working situations, to emotional intelligence helps more than one's intellectual potential or even professional skills and competencies. A professionally competent person having poor emotional intelligence may suffer on account of his inability to deal with his self or getting along properly with others. For handling mental relationships, emotional intelligence is very much needed.

Rationale for the Study

A higher secondary student cannot be an exception to this fact. In the case of a higher secondary student, in all sense his emotional intelligence essentially reflects his ability to deal successfully with other students and with his own feelings. These qualities count significantly towards his success in his area of achievement.

Emotional intelligence as a unitary ability is helpful in knowing, feeling and judging emotions in close co-operation with one's thinking process to behave in a proper way for the ultimate realise of the happiness and welfare of the self and to deal with his students.

The investigator had informal chats with the higher secondary commerce students and come to know about the extent of possession of emotional intelligence. He came to know that many students did not possess adequate emotional intelligence to achieve high marks in Commerce subject that would help them to become successful cost accountants, chartered accountants, banking professionals etc., and prepare the higher secondary commerce students for a bright future of the nation. Under these circumstances, the investigator has decided to undertake an investigation on the emotional intelligence of the higher secondary commerce students.

Objectives

General Objective

To analyse the emotional intelligence of higher secondary commerce students in Tiruchendur Taluk in relation to their academic achievement.

Specific Objectives

1. To analyse the emotional intelligence of higher secondary commerce students in Tiruchendur Taluk in terms of (1) Class – XI and XII (2) Nature of School – Unisex and Co-education.
2. To analyse the academic achievement of higher secondary commerce students in terms of (1) Class – XI and XII (2) Nature of School – Unisex and Co-education.
3. To analyse the relationship between emotional intelligence and academic achievement of higher secondary commerce students in terms of (1) Class – XI and XII (2) Nature of School – Unisex and Co-education.

Population and Sample

The population of the present study consists of all the higher secondary students studying in commerce group in the higher secondary schools of Tiruchendur Taluk.

The investigator has selected 358 students from five different schools of Tiruchendur Taluk through stratified random sampling technique.

Research Method used for the Study

The investigator adopts the survey method of research to study the emotional intelligence of higher secondary commerce students in Tiruchendur taluk.

Tools Employed in the Study

1. Emotional Intelligence Scale developed by Dr. S. Arockiasamy (2006).
2. Half-year marks of the Commerce students.

Statistical Techniques Employed in the Study

The following statistical techniques was to be adopted for the study: (1) Mean (2) Standard Deviation (3) 't' test (4) Product Moment Correlation.

Findings

Table 23.1: Difference in Emotional Intelligence of Higher Secondary Commerce Students with Reference to Class

Emotional Intelligence	Class	N	Mean	SD	Calculated 't' value	Remark
Self-awareness	XI	170	20.52	3.59	1.98	NS
	XII	188	21.34	4.20		
Self-regulation	XI	170	18.25	4.18	1.15	NS
	XII	188	18.82	5.11		
Motivation	XI	170	19.99	3.86	1.55	NS
	XII	188	20.70	4.75		
Empathy	XI	170	19.43	4.61	1.09	NS
	XII	188	19.96	4.56		
Social Skills	XI	170	18.70	4.48	0.52	NS
	XII	188	18.44	5.11		
Total	XI	170	96.90	16.48	1.22	NS
	XII	188	99.26	20.15		

(Table value 't' = 1.96 at 0.05% Level)

Since the calculated 't' values are less than the table value for 356 degrees of freedom at 5 per cent level of significance, the null hypothesis is accepted with reference to emotional intelligence and its dimensions – self-regulation, motivation, empathy and social skills.

Since the calculated 't' value is greater than the table value for 356 degrees of freedom at 5 per cent level of significance, the null hypothesis is rejected with reference to the dimension – self-awareness.

Table 23.2: Difference in Emotional Intelligence of Higher Secondary Commerce Students with Reference to Nature of School

Emotional Intelligence	School Nature	N	Mean	SD	Calculated 't' value	Table Value	Remark
Self-awareness	Unisex	173	20.69	3.89	1.23	1.96	NS
	Co-ed.	185	21.20	3.98			
Self-regulation	Unisex	173	18.49	5.15	0.23	1.96	NS
	Co-ed.	185	18.61	4.25			
Motivation	Unisex	173	19.73	4.60	2.69	1.96	S
	Co-ed.	185	20.96	4.03			
Empathy	Unisex	173	19.72	4.98	0.04	1.96	NS
	Co-ed.	185	19.70	4.20			
Social Skills	Unisex	173	18.36	4.86	0.77	1.96	NS
	Co-ed.	185	18.75	4.77			
Total	Unisex	173	96.98	19.97	1.14	1.96	NS
	Co-ed.	185	99.22	17.01			

Since the calculated 't' values are less than the table value for 356 degrees of freedom at 5 per cent level of significance, the null hypothesis is accepted with reference to emotional intelligence and its dimensions – self-awareness, self-regulation, empathy and social skills.

Since the calculated 't' value is greater than the table value for 356 degrees of freedom at 5 per cent level of significance, the null hypothesis is rejected with reference to the dimension – motivation.

Table 23.3: Difference in Achievement of Higher Secondary Commerce Students with Reference to Class

Class	N	Mean	SD	Calculated 't' value	Table Value	Remark
XI	170	93.27	30.89	6.78	1.96	S
XII	188	116.99	35.32			

Since the calculated 't' value is greater than the table value for 356 degrees of freedom at 5 per cent level of significance, the null hypothesis is rejected.

Table 23.4: Difference in Achievement of Higher Secondary Commerce Students with Reference to Nature of School

Nature of the School	N	Mean	SD	Calculated 't' value	Table Value	Remark
Unisex	173	113.63	39.98	2.52	1.96	S
Co-educational	185	102.49	32.73			

Since the calculated 't' value is greater than the table value for 356 degrees of freedom at 5 per cent level of significance, the null hypothesis is rejected.

Table 23.5: Relationship between Emotional Intelligence and Achievement of Higher Secondary Commerce Students with Reference to Background Variables

Variable	Category	N	Calculated 'r' value	Table Value	Remark
Class	XI	170	-0.111	0.151	NS
	XII	188	-0.139	0.144	NS
	Private	254	-0.090	0.125	NS
Nature of School	Unisex	173	-0.041	0.150	NS
	Co-ed.	185	-0.159	0.145	S
	Joint	24	0.134	0.404	NS

Since the calculated 'r' values are less than the table values at 5 per cent level of significance, the null hypothesis is accepted with reference to class and nature of school (unisex).

Since the calculated 'r' values are greater than the table values at 5 per cent level of significance, the null hypothesis is rejected with reference to nature of school which is co-educational.

Conclusion

From the findings of the present study, the investigator found that significant relationship is found between the emotional intelligence and achievement in commerce of higher secondary co-education students, schools. From this, emotional intelligence is a deciding factor for the achievement in commerce subject. Generally speaking, emotionally well-balanced students are able to face their problems in an effective manner and able to find the solutions to the problems easily.

These things will motivate the students in their academic achievement. Hence, the investigator concluded that emotional intelligence is an essential factor that should persist in any student for achieving his/her ultimate target.

REFERENCES

Aggarwal, J. C. (1966). Educational Research: An Introduction, Arya Book Depot, New Delhi.

Barr, A. S., Davis, R. A. and Johnson (1953). Educational Research – An Appraisal, J. B. Lippon Cot Co., Chicago.

Clifford T. Morgan, Richard A. King, John R.Weiz and John Scholpler (1993). Introduction to Psychology, Tata McGraw Hill Publishing Co. Ltd., New Delhi.

Good V. Carter, A. S. Barr and Doughlas E. Scates (1935). Methodology of Educational Research, Appleton Century Crafts Inc., New York.

Good, Barr and Scates (1941). Essentials of Educational Research: Methodology and Design, Appleton Century Crafts, New York.

John W. Best (1995). Research in Education, Prentice Hall of India Pvt. Ltd., New Delhi.

Page 170-179

Recent Trend in Educational Research
Edited by: **Dr. D. Sivakumar**
Edition: **2015**
ISBN: 978-93-5056-741-8
Published by: **Discovery Publishing House Pvt. Ltd., New Delhi (India)**

24

Influence of Self-concept on Academic Achievement of D.T.Ed Students

S. Devadoss Vasantharaj

INTRODUCTION

Self-concept is one the dominant factors of personality. Good self-concept becomes the positive hope for an individual. It means how one thinks or feels about oneself and one's evaluation of one's own abilities and attributes. Students with a positive self-concept tend to be confident and assertive in their judgement and abilities. Students with a negative self-concept are described as: quiet, unoriginal, lacking in initiative, withdrawn and so on (Copper Smith, 1967). In our culture, achievement is one of the most common ways of enhancing the self-concept. In educational psychology, the term achievement applies specified level of proficiency in academic work in general or a specific skill such as: reading, writing or arithmetic. There has been a growing tendency to explore personality factors in the academic performance. Investigations so far undertaken have covered variety of personality traits like persistence, anxiety, emotion, memory, values, mental health, interest and so on. These studies reveal

Ph.D. Scholar, Bharatiyar University, Coimbatore.

that these personality traits certainly influence the academic achievement of the students.

'Self-concept' has been defined as the individual's way of looking at himself. It also signifies his way of thinking, feeling and behaving (Saraswat and Gaur, 1981).

Academic achievement has been defined as: "the knowledge attained and skill developed in the school subjects which are usually determined by test scores or by marks assigned by teacher or both" (Good, 1959).

According to Block A. M. (1978), "Achievement refers to the level of proficiency of an individual in some walks of activity or subject matter. Achievement is a task oriented behaviour that allows the individual performance to be evaluated".

Significance of the Study

A person's view of himself/herself or his/her self-concept is closely related to how he/she behaves and learns. It is understood that a student's performance depends not only on how bright he/she actually is but also on how bright he/she feels he/she is. Thus student's self-concept is a functional and a facilitating factor in their achievement. Achievement of students is the prime concern of teachers, teacher-educators and psychologists. Research investigators have been busy identifying and investigating various factors influencing achievement. The importance of achievement has raised several important questions in educational researches. What are the factors which facilitate and retard achievement in students? And how far do the different factors contribute towards difference in achievement? Is there a difference between expected outcomes of educator and the real outcomes? Thus the nature of education itself demands research in its various areas. Nowadays as against the previous concept of assigning major roles to cognitive variables, more emphasis is laid on affective outcomes of education like development of self-concept, interest and so on. So in the present study, the investigator makes an attempt to study the influence of self-concept on academic achievement.

Objectives of the Study

This study has been undertaken with the following objectives in mind:

1. To study the level of self-concept of D.T.Ed students.
2. To study the level of academic achievement of D.T.Ed students.
3. To find out the relationship between self-concept and academic achievement of D.T.Ed students.
4. To find out the difference if any, in the level of self-concept between:
   - Boys and Girls,
   - Students with Urban and Rural background.
5. To find out the difference if any, in the level of academic achievement between:
   - Boys and Girls,
   - Students with Urban and Rural background.

Hypotheses of the Study

The following hypotheses have been framed to attain the above said objectives:

1. The level of self-concept and academic achievement of D.T.Ed Students are not high.
2. There is no significant relationship between self-concept and academic achievement of D.T.Ed Students.
3. Boys and Girls do not differ significantly in their level of self-concept.
4. Students with rural and urban background do not differ significantly in their level of self-concept.
5. Boys and Girls do not differ significantly in their level academic achievement.
6. Students with rural and urban background do not differ significantly in their level academic achievement.

Research Methodology

In order to achieve the objectives of the present investigation, survey method was used. The methodological details like sample, tool, procedure of data collection, scoring procedure and statistical techniques are given below:

Sample

The sample of present study consists of 300 D.T.Ed students of Karaikal region and was drawn through random sampling technique.

Tool Used

To study the influence of self-concept on the academic achievement of the students, the self-concept questionnaire standardized by Raj Kumar Saraswat (1984) was used. To study the academic achievement the term exam (in percentage) was taken as the achievement score.

Data Collection

In order to assess the self-concept of the students, the questionnaire was distributed to them and administered faithfully in strict accordance with the directions provided in the manual for testing procedure.

Statistical Technique Used

In order to analyze and interpret data, the following statistical techniques were used: descriptive analysis, correlational analysis and differential analysis.

Analysis and Interpretation of Data

For analysis and interpretation of data the study has been analyzed in different tables. The same is presented here.

Table 24.1: Mean and Standard Deviation for Self-concept and Academic Achievement Score of whole Group

Categories	Number	Mean	Standard Deviation
Self-concept	300	180.08	14.01
Academic Achievement	300	54.3	17.91

From Table 24.1, it is found that the mean of total self-concept scores is 180.08 with a standard deviation of 14.01. It is observed that an individual can score a maximum of 240. So it is inferred that the self-concept of D.T.Ed students is high. Hence hypothesis No. 1 that the level of self-concept of D.T.Ed Students is not high is rejected.

It is found from the same Table 24.1 that the mean of total academic achievement scores is 54.3 with a standard deviation of 17.91. It is observed that an individual can score a maximum of 100. Hence it is inferred that the academic achievement of D.T.Ed students is average. Hence hypothesis No. 1 that the level of academic achievement of D.T.Ed Students is not high is accepted.

Table 24.2: Relationship between Self-concept and Academic Achievement

Sl. No.	Categories	Df	'r'	Significant Level 0.01
1.	Self-concept	298	0.19	S
2.	Academic Achievement			

S - Significant

From Table 24.2 it is found that there is a positive relationship between self-concept and academic achievement at 0.01 level of significance. Hence, the null hypothesis that there is no relationship between self-concept and academic achievement of D.T.Ed students is rejected.

Table 24.3: Mean, Standard Deviation and 't' value for Self-concept Scores of Boys and Girls

Self-concept	Boys N=125		Girls N=175		MD	't' value	Significant Level
	Mean	SD	Mean	SD			
(A)Physical	28.97	3.73	28.70	3.04	0.27	0.43	NS
(B)Social	30.09	3.60	30.31	2.89	0.22	0.36	NS
(C)Temperamental	28.86	3.73	29.62	3.30	0.76	1.19	NS
(D)Educational	31.81	4.51	32.70	4.69	0.89	1.21	NS
(E)Moral	31.76	3.57	33.87	3.04	2.11	3.41	S (0.01)
(F)Intellectual	27.48	4.23	26.45	3.56	1.03	1.53	NS
Total	178.97	15.08	181.65	12.24	2.68	2.13	S (0.05)

S – Significant, NS – Not Significant

It can be observed in Table 24.3 that girls are significantly superior to boys in element E (Moral). In other elements, the differences between the mean scores are very small and not significant. The overall self-concept mean score of girls (181.65) is greater than the overall self-concept mean score of boys

(178.97). Hence, girls have more self-concept than boys. Since it is found that gender brings variations in overall self-concept, there is a significant difference between the gender in terms of their self-concept. The calculated 't' value is greater than the table value for df = 298 at 0.05 level of significance for overall self-concept. Hence, the null hypothesis that boys and girls do not differ significantly in their level of self-concept is rejected.

Table 24.4: Mean, Standard Deviation and 't' value for Self-concept of Urban and Rural Students

Self-concept	Urban N=175		Rural N=125		MD	't' value	Significant Level 0.05
	Mean	SD	Mean	SD			
(A)Physical	28.74	3.70	29.01	3.08	0.27	0.43	NS
(B)Social	29.82	3.43	30.69	3.10	0.87	1.41	NS
(C)Temperamental	28.73	3.75	29.81	3.22	1.08	1.70	NS
(D)Educational	32.67	4.36	31.50	4.85	1.17	1.59	NS
(E)Moral	31.99	3.79	33.55	2.85	1.56	2.52	S
(F)Intellectual	27.09	4.47	27.00	3.21	0.09	0.14	NS
Total	179.03	15.56	181.55	11.39	2.52	2.02	S

S – Significant, NS – Not Significant

It is evident from Table 24.4 that rural students are significantly superior to urban students in element E (Moral). Differences in mean scores of total self-concept are also in favour of rural students. In other elements the differences between the mean scores are not significant. The overall self-concept mean score of rural students (181.55) are greater than the overall self-concept mean score of urban students (179.03). Hence, rural students have more self-concept than urban students. Since it is found that locality brings variations in overall self-concept, there is a significant difference between the locality of the students and their self-concept. The calculated 't' value is greater than the table value for df = 298 at 0.05 level of significance for over all self-concept. Hence, the null hypothesis that students with rural and urban background do not differ significantly in their level of self-concept is rejected.

Table 24.5: 't' value for Mean Scores of Academic Achievement of Boys and Girls

Categories	Number	Mean	S.D	't' value	Significant Level 0.01
Boys	125	49.33	18.97	8.61	S
Girls	175	61.15	13.64		

S = Significant

It is evident from 't' value 8.61 mentioned in Table 24.5 that the difference between means of scores obtained in academic achievement by boys and girls is significant at 0.01 level. Since the mean (49.33) level of score obtained by the boys is lower than that of girls (61.15). The 't' test was applied to find out whether the difference is significant or not. Table 24.5 shows that the 't' value is higher than the table value. It may be concluded that girls have significantly higher academic achievement than boys. There is a significant difference between the groups. Hence, the null hypothesis that boys and girls do not differ significantly in their level academic achievement is rejected.

Table 24.6: 't' value for Mean Scores of Academic Achievement of Students with Rural and Urban Background

Categories	Number	Mean	S.D	't' value	Significant Level 0.01
Urban	175	55.52	16.98	2.07	S
Rural	125	52.49	19.06		

S = Significant

It is evident from 't' value 2.07 mentioned in Table 24.6 that the difference between means of scores obtained in academic achievement by students with urban and rural background is significant at 0.05 level. Mean (55.52) level of score obtained by the urban students is greater than that of rural students (52.49). The't' test was applied to find out whether the difference is significant or not. Table 24.6 shows that the 't' value is higher than the table value. It may be concluded that urban students have significantly higher academic achievement than rural students. There is a significant difference between the groups.

Hence, the null hypothesis that students with rural and urban background do not differ significantly in their level academic achievement is rejected.

Findings of the Study

- The result of the study indicates that the level of self-concept of the D.T.Ed students is high.
- The academic achievement of the D.T.Ed students is not too high and not too low.
- There is significant positive relationship between self-concept and academic achievement of D.T.Ed students.
- Boys and girls differ significantly in their level of self-concept and the level of academic achievement.
- Students with rural and urban background differ significantly in their level of self-concept.
- Students with rural and urban background differ significantly in their level of academic achievement.

Results and Discussion

It is understood from the perusal of the study that there is significant positive relationship between self-concept and academic achievement of D.T.Ed students. It is inferred from the present study that the Self concept of D.T.Ed students in Karaikal region is high but their Academic Achievement is average. It is also observed that girls have high self-concept than boys. It is interesting to note that students with rural background have higher self-concept than with urban background. It is concluded from the above discussion that self-concept has significant effects on academic achievement of D.T.Ed students. The present study emphasizes the necessity to develop the self-concept of D.T.Ed students, which in turn helps to develop their academic achievement. If the classroom activities do not enhance the students' positive self-concept, their academic achievement will go down.

The following recommendations are suggested by the investigator to improve the level of self-concept of the students:

1. Self-concept of the students on their intellectual status can be built up by introducing creative work, problem solving games, essay contests, debates, quiz and group discussions on a large scale in training institutes.

2. Associations/clubs should be formed in various subjects and each student must be assigned with some responsibility. This would enhance their self-concept.
3. Various types of functions and extra-curricular programmes should be organized frequently, which would provide excellent opportunities for sharing responsibilities and thereby helping them to acquire self-concept.
4. Educational psychologists and counsellors can help students develop positive self-concept towards them. Teachers, psychologists and educational planners should evolve concrete measures that will prove conducive in inculcating positive self-concept among students.
5. Counselling services should be arranged for students for improving their self-image.
6. Since teachers play a vital role in the student's self-concept on intellectual and academic status, short-term courses/ summer institutions/ lectures in human behaviour…etc., shall be arranged in a fruitful manner.
7. Congenial atmosphere in training institutes should be evolved. Facilitating the students' ability to draw his/her feelings. To face his/her feeling, to experience life comfortably should be a part of the educational experience.

REFERENCES

Amy M. Gans, (2003). Comparing the Self-Concept of Students With and Without Learning Disabilities, University of Miami, *Journal of Learning Disabilities*, Vol. 36, No. 3, 287-295, Florida.

Chandra S. S and Renu Roa., (2006). "Educational Psychology, Evaluation and Statistics", Surya Publications, Meerut.

House J.D., (2000), Achievement – Related Expectancies, Academic Self-concept, and Mathematics Performance of Academically under Prepared Adolescent Students, *Office of Institutional Research, Northern Illinois University*.

Muijs, R. D., (1997). Predictors of Academic Achievement and Academic Self-Concept: A Longitudinal Perspective, *British Journal of Educational Psychology* 67: 263-277.

Mimi Bong; Richard E. Clark, (1999). Comparison between Self-concept and Self-efficacy in Academic Motivation Research, *Educational Psychologist*, Volume 34, Issue 3, p. 139-153, USA.

Teresa L. Hunt, (1997), Self-concept, Hope and Achievement: A Look at the Relationship between the Individual Self-concept, Level of Hope, and Academic Achievement, Missouri Western State College.

Page 180-186
Recent Trend in Educational Research
Edited by: **Dr. D. Sivakumar**
Edition: **2015**
ISBN: 978-93-5056-741-8
Published by: **Discovery Publishing House Pvt. Ltd., New Delhi (India)**

25

A Study Habits and Achievement of IX Standard Studetns in Namakkal District

M. Balasupramaniam

INTRODUCTION

Today we are living in a world of science and technology, which with the explosion of knowledge during the last few decades is fast approaching towards a technocratic-age. Hence, each individual needs to prepare himself to live effectively and contribute meaningfully with time. How to achieve this? The answer lies in attaining academic excellence. It is very important for the young. Education is the chief means through which we can acquire the academic excellence and also learn to adjust to our environment. Education is one of the important enterprises, which involves students at every stage and level. The students who are part and parcel of education process often do not know how to utilize their time properly. Poor study habits are one of the important causes of educational backwardness. The potential of any one for full scholastic achievement is hardly even realized due to many factors. Attempts need be made to remove obstacles to attain higher education by improving the quality of instruction,

Ph.D. Scholar, Bharatiyar University, Coimbatore.

instructional material, educational environment, and so on. On the part of the students also, attempts need be made to improve their motivation, interest and work habits so that they can maximize their potential.

Need for the Study

The teaching-learning process involves a simultaneous mutual exchange of ideas and interaction between the teachers and taught where besides the teacher; the learner has to organize himself for work, to do the assigned work, to solve-problems and to make decisions which reveal something about his unique study habits. There are major differences in the study habits form one student to another and those differences can have a significant bearing on the totality of learning. Unless a teacher can pinpoint exactly 'what' a child needs to study and 'how' he could develop study habits too establish a most successful pattern of studying any attempt on individualized instruction is like a shot in the dark.

Statement of the Problem

A Study Habits and Achievement of IX Std. Students in Namakkal District.

Objectives

General Objectives

To analyze the study habits and achievement of IX std. Students in Namakkal District.

Specific Objectives

1. To analyze the study habits of IX std. Students in terms of Gender (Male\Female), Religion (Hindu\Non-Hindu) and Community (BC\others).
2. To analyze the achievement of IX std. Students in terms of Gender (Male\Female), Religion (Hindu\Non-Hindu) and Community (BC\others).

Hypotheses of the Study

1. There is no significant difference between the mean scores of study habits of male and female IX standard students.
2. There is no significant difference between the mean scores of study habits of Hindu and Non-Hindu IX standard students.

3. There is no significant difference between the mean scores of study habits of BC and Non-BC IX standard students.
4. There is no significant difference between the mean scores of achievement of male and female IX standard students.
5. There is no significant difference between the mean scores of achievement of Hindu and Non-Hindu IX standard students.
6. There is no significant difference between the mean scores of achievement of BC and Non-BC IX standard students.

Method Adopted in the Present Study

The investigator has selected survey method in the present study. Survey is a method in which data are systematically collected from a population through some form of direct solicitation such as presenting of questionnaires, interviews, etc., the investigator used stratified random sampling technique for studying the relationship between study habits and achievement of IX std. Students.

Tools used in the Present Study

1. Study habits inventory scale developed the standardized by Dr. Gopal Rao (1990).
2. Half-yearly exam marks of IX std. Students.

In the present study, the investigator has chosen standardized tool for assessing the study habits of IX STD students in Namakkal District.

Establishing Reliability

Even though the tool was standardized to find out whether the tool was reliable to the sample selected, the investigator has employed the test-retest method to establish reliability. The tool was translated into Tamil and administered to 30 students selected randomly in the in the Mahindra Matriculation School, Kumaramangalam. After a week, the same tool was given to the same set of the students. Both the responses were scored and analyzed. The computed co-efficient for the test and retest is 0.71. Thus the reliability was established.

Population

According to John W. Best and James V. Khan (1992), "A Population is any group of individuals that have one or more characteristics in common that are if interest to the researcher. The population may be all the individuals of a particular type, or a more restricted part of that group". The population of the present study comprises all the higher schools students in Tiruchengode Taluk in Namakkal District.

Sample

According to S. K. Gupta 1994 "A sample consists of a small collection from some larger aggregate about which we wish information. He further states, "It is the sample that we observe but it is the population which we seek to know". The investigator has selected 210 students from six different higher secondary schools in Tiruchengodu Taluk of Namakkal District through Stratified random sample technique.

Administration of the Tool

To collect data, the investigator visited the higher Secondary Schools in Tiruchengodu Taluk of Namakkal District. The investigator got the consent of the heads as well as the teachers of the students. He explained the tool to the students. He requested the students to answer all the questions and return them in a complete manner. After 30 minutes, he collected all the filled up questionnaires. Thus the tool was administered.

Statistical Methods

For the present study, the investigator has used Mean, Standard Deviation and 't' test the statistical techniques.

Null Hypothesis No. 1

There is no significant difference between the mean scores of study habits of male and female IX standard students.

Table 25.1:

Sex	N	M	SD	SE_d	$M_1 - M_2$	Df	't'
Male	125	143.40	22.27	3.019	2.90	208	0.981*
Female	85	146.31	20.24				

*Not Significant at 0.05 level.

From Table 25.1 it is inferred that the calculated 't' value .981 is less that the table value (1.96) at 5 per cent level for 208 degrees of freedom. Hence the null hypothesis is accepted. There is no significant difference between the mean scores of study habits of male and female IX standard students.

Null Hypothesis No. 2

There is no significant difference between the mean scores of study habits of Hindu and Non-Hindu IX standard students.

Table 25.2:

Religion	N	M	SD	SE_d	$M_1 - M_2$	Df	't'
Hindu	153	144.33	21.59	3.33	.905	208	0.273*
Non-Hindu	57	145.24	21.33				

*Not Significant at 0.05 level.

From Table 25.2 it is inferred that the calculated 't' value .273 is less that the table value (1.96) at 5 per cent level for 208 degrees of freedom. Hence the null hypothesis is accepted. There is no significant difference between the mean scores of study habits of Hindu and Non-Hindu IX standard students.

Null Hypotheses No. 3

There is no significant difference between the mean scores of study habits of BC and Non-BC IX standard students.

Table 25.3:

Community	N	M	SD	SE_d	$M_1 - M_2$	Df	't'
BC	148	144.12	23.61	3.254	1.549	208	0.564*
Non-BC	62	145.67	15.32				

*Not Significant at 0.05 level.

From Table 25.3 it is inferred that the calculated 't' value .564 is less that the table value (1.96) at 5 per cent level for 208 degrees of freedom. Hence the null hypothesis is accepted. There is no significant difference between the mean scores of study habits of BC and Non-BC IX standard students.

Null Hypothesis No. 4

There is no significant difference between the mean scores of achievement of male and female IX standard students.

Table 25.4:

Sex	N	M	SD	SE_d	$M_1 - M_2$	Df	't'
Male	125	58.39	17.54	2.24	1.13	208	0.506*
Female	85	59.53	14.77				

*Not Significant at 0.05 level.

From Table 25.4 it is inferred that the calculated 't' value .506 is less that the table value (1.96) at 5 per cent level for 208 degrees of freedom. Hence the null hypothesis is accepted. That is, there is no significant difference between the mean scores of achievement of male and female IX standard students.

Null Hypothesis No. 5

There is no significant difference between the mean scores of achievement of Hindu and Non-Hindu IX standard students.

Table 25.5:

Religion	N	M	SD	SE_d	$M_1 - M_2$	Df	't'
Hindu	153	59.04	17.01	2.41	.694	208	0.288*
Non-Hindu	57	58.34	14.97				

*Not Significant at 0.05 level.

From Table 25.5 it is inferred that the calculated 't' value .288 is less that the table value (1.96) at 5 per cent level for 208 degrees of freedom. Hence the null hypothesis is accepted. That is, there is no significant difference between the mean scores of achievement of Hindu and Non-Hindu IX standard students.

Null Hypothesis No. 6

There is no significant difference between the mean scores of achievement of BC and Non-BC IX standard students.

Table 25.6:

Community	N	M	SD	SE_d	$M_1 - M_2$	Df	't'
BC	148	59.75	15.50	2.67	3.05	208	1.14*
Non-BC	62	56.70	18.47				

*Not Significant at 0.05 level.

From Table 25.6 it is inferred that the calculated 't' value 1.14 is less that the table value (.96) at 5 per cent level for 208 degrees of freedom. Hence the null hypothesis is accepted. That is, there is no significant difference between the mean scores of achievement of BC and Non-BC IX standard students.

Major Findings

1. There is no significant difference between the mean scores of study habits of male and female.
2. There is no significant difference between the mean scores of study habits of Hindu and Non-Hindu IX standard students.
3. There is no significant difference between the mean scores of study habits of BC and Non-BC IX standard students.
4. There is no significant difference between the mean scores of achievement of male and female IX standard students.
5. There is no significant difference between the mean scores of achievement of Hindu and Non-Hindu IX standard students.
6. There is no significant difference between the mean scores of achievement of BC and Non-BC IX standard students.

Educational Implications of the Study

The study reveals that there is no significant difference between the variables as far as the gender, Religion, Caste is concerened, and so it is obivious that the students are having good study habit along with their academic achievement irrespective of gender, Caste, Community. It is due to their academic focus which may be inculcated by their teachers as well as by their parents.

REFERENCES

Jamuar, K. K. (1974). Study Habits of College Students, Indian International Publications, Allahabad.

Mangal, S. K. (1997). Educational Psychology Prakash Brothers, Ludhiana.

Patel, M. R. (1997). "Study Habits of Pupil and its Impact upon their Academic Achievement, the Progress of Education, Pune vidyarthi Griha Prakashan, Vol. LXXL, No. 6, January 1997.

Page 187-191
Recent Trend in Educational Research
***Edited by:* Dr. D. Sivakumar**
***Edition:* 2015**
ISBN: 978-93-5056-741-8
***Published by:* Discovery Publishing House Pvt. Ltd., New Delhi (India)**

26

Effectiveness of Computer Assisted Instruction (CAI) in Teaching XI Physics

Selvi Jeya Ruby

INTRODUCTION

The demands from science education vary from time to time. There has been great explosion of knowledge during the last few decades. The main tasks of education in a modern society are to keep pace with the rate of increasing knowledge and this knowledge cannot be received passively. The main account in education should be on the awakening of curiosity, the simulations of creativity, the development of proper interests, attitudes and values and building of essential skills such as: independent study, capacity to think, judge for oneself etc.

Computer Assisted Instruction

The greatest contribution of present day technology is the development of Computer Assisted Instruction (CAI), which has proved an efficient and effective media in education. But in our country, we have introduced computer to such limited areas as data processing and decision-making only.

Ph.D. Scholar, Bharatiyar University, Coimbatore.

Need and Importance of the Study

For effective teaching, the teachers need in-depth knowledge and insights to teach fundamental concepts in the discipline. Teaching Physics has its own special requirements that teachers find difficult to meet. Computers have the potential to increase the effectiveness of teaching Physics.

Computer technology has vast potential as an effective teaching aid and computers can perform simulations of experiments, give multimedia presentations and offer interactive methods such as: online quizzes. Further more, the Internet is a source of great ideas, lesson plan for teaching of various units, and it contains interesting additional information.

A further development is that Computers have become very user friendly. Teachers are receiving basic training in the use of Computers. General purpose and easy to use slide show software such as: Microsoft Power point has, for the first time, made it possible for the teachers themselves to easily modify and even provide their own slides based on the needs of their own classes. Hence, the investigator felt that there is a need to develop computer assisted instruction and to study its effectiveness.

Objectives of the Study

1. To develop Computer Assisted Instruction package in three different modes *viz;* Simulation, Tutorial, Drill and Practice for the selected contents of XI Standard Physics Text-book of Tamil Nadu.
2. To find out whether there is any significant difference between the traditional lecture method and Computer Assisted Instruction in terms of their effectiveness.
3. To find out whether there is any significant difference between Simulation, Tutorial and Drill and Practice modes of Computer Assisted Instruction and conventional method on the achievement of XI standard students in Physics subject.

Hypotheses of the Study

1. There is no significant difference between the traditional lecture method and Computer Assisted Instruction in terms of their effectiveness.

2. There is no significant difference between the traditional lecture method and Computer Assisted Instruction in Simulation mode in terms of their effectiveness.
3. There is no significant difference between the traditional lecture method and Computer Assisted Instruction in Tutorial mode in terms of their effectiveness.
4. There is no significant difference between the traditional lecture method and Computer Assisted Instruction in Drill and practice mode in terms of their effectiveness.

Method of Study

The present investigation was undertaken by using the experimental method with control and experimental groups. The difference between these two group's achievements indicates the effectiveness of CAI. For this study Computer Assisted Instruction programme with Simulation, Tutorial and Drill and Practice modes were prepared using Flash software. The Control Group was taught with traditional-lecture method and the experimental group was taught with CAI (each unit with one of the modes of CAI). An achievement test was conducted for the three units, for the control and experimental groups. The scores were statistically treated to find out the effectiveness.

Tools used in this Study

The Investigators of the present study has chosen the following tools for data collection.

1. Computer Assisted Instruction package in three different modes for selected Units of XI Standard Physics.
2. Achievement test in Physics subject for the selected three units of XI Standard Physics.

Statistical Techniques used

In this present investigation the following statistical techniques were used.

1. Descriptive analysis:
   (a) Measure of central tendency (Mean).
   (b) Measure of variability (Standard Deviation).

2. Differential analysis:
   (*a*) 't' test (to find the level of significance).

Procedure

The sample was taken from Thandhai Periyar Government Higher Secondary School of Karaikal, of Puducherry. The present study consists of 120 samples for need of identification phase. In which 30 + 30 = 60 students were taken as samples (Control Group N = 30, Experimental Group N = 30) for the final study based on the scores obtained by them in the pre-test.

These two groups were taught with traditional method of teaching and different modes CAI. Then a post-test was conducted to find out their achievement in each unit and the relative effectiveness among different modes of CAI.

Statistical Analysis

Table 26.1: Significance of Difference between the Means of the Control and Experimental Groups on the Achievement Scores in Physics

Mode of CAI	Control		Experimental		't' value	Remarks at 0.5 Level
	Mean	S.D	Mean	S.D		
Simulation	13.36	2.07	15.30	2.24	3.46	Significant
Drill and Practice	13.73	2.27	15.06	2.28	3.11	Significant
Tutorial	13.33	2.29	15.83	2.52	4.01	Significant
CAI	40.43	2.63	46.70	4.58	6.48	Significant

Table 26.1 shows that among different modes of CAI teaching (46.70) is greater than the control group. Hence the null hypothesis is rejected. As the 't' values shows that there is a significance difference between traditional way of teaching and simulation, drill and practice and tutorial method of teaching. Hence the Null Hypotheses were rejected. Table 26.1 shows that, achievement means of Tutorial mode (15.83) was better than all other two modes; Drill and Practice (15.06) and Simulation (15.30) of CAI. In total; experimental group mean (46.70) was better than Control group.

Important Findings and Interpretation

1. Among the three different modes of teaching like Simulation, Tutorial, and Drill and Practice of CAI, mode Tutorial mode of CAI teaching shows a higher achievement than all other modes of CAI teaching.
2. In total the traditional method of teaching with CAI; CAI method of teaching shows higher achievement than conventional method of teaching.

This study on CAI shows its effectiveness than the conventional lecture method of teaching and among different modes (Simulation, Tutorial, and Drill and Practice) of CAI Tutorial mode shows high achievement than all other modes of CAI. This shows the need and importance of CAI for Physics teaching.

Recommendations

1. As the result shows the effectiveness of CAI and in particular of CAI, Software packages for all the lessons may be prepared.
2. User friendly software may be identified and by providing computer training to the teachers this technology may be utilized further effectively.

REFERENCES

Arthur B. Goodwin (1969). Handbook of Audio-Visual Aids and Techniques for Teaching Elementary School Subjects West Nyack N-Y., Parker Publishing Company.

Lawson, R. and de Matos, C. (2000). Information Technology Skills in the Workplace: Implications for Bachelor of Arts Degrees. *Australian Journal of Education*, 16(2), 87-103.

Aggarwal, Y. P. (1986). Statistical Methods: Concepts, Application and Computation, New Delhi: Sterling Publisher Pvt Ltd.

Page 192-201

Recent Trend in Educational Research
Edited by: **Dr. D. Sivakumar**
Edition: **2015**
ISBN: 978-93-5056-741-8
Published by: **Discovery Publishing House Pvt. Ltd., New Delhi (India)**

27

A Study on Integrating Information and Communication Technology in Teacher Education

P. S. Jayasree

INTRODUCTION

The world is changing rapid and the growth of knowledge is phenomenal. To cope up with this rapid change need for a change in its present system of education, as yesterday's education system will not meet today's need, and even less, the needs for tomorrow. As education is the key to the national prosperity and welfare, it is essential that it should change rapidly. According to John Dewey (1976) "Education is the development of all those capacities in the individual, which will enable him to control his environment and fulfill his possibilities". The future of a nation is fashioned in a classroom. Education is a socially oriented activity which is associated with strong teachers having high degrees of personal control with learners.

A teacher plays an important role in the process of Education. A teacher is considered to be the architect of the nation. In other words, the future of the nation lies in the hands of a teacher. Aristotle rightly says: "Those who educate

Ph.D. Scholar, Bharatiyar University, Coimbatore.

children well are more to the honoured than they who produce them; for these only gave them life, those art of living well". According to Verma (2010), a teacher plays a significant role not only in class teaching learning situation but in social engineering too.

A teacher acts as a facility centre of information and knowledge. A teacher after gathering information from specified sources like text books, personal notes, library etc., communicates it to the students. Not only has this teacher developed the quality of creativity in students. A teacher arises a passion for the subject among the students by getting them to look at issues in a variety of ways. A teacher instills a hunger in their students to learn more on their own which strengthens the good future of students.

Role of ICT in Education

It is well accepted fact that a single teacher cannot provide the complete and up-to-date information in any subject ICT can fill this gap as it provide access to different sources of information. Educational institution is also in the midst of information waves. Instead of big schools are emerged. Accordingly, the duties and responsibilities of the teachers and learners are to be changed to adjust with the new society at the new environment.

Need for Study

Education in India has undergone various phases and stages of development starting from the Gurukula system of education in the Vedic age to the new system of education in the post-independent period. At all stages of development there was a concern for bringing in quality education on the practical aspects in education.

The great Indian thinkers had emphasized on developing the inner potential of individuals by reflecting upon unique potential of individuals. Getting educated is solely dependent upon the individual teacher's role to set conditions and generate environments for learning. Traditionally, the teacher used to be the complete source of knowledge for the students. But now, in many cases, the teachers do not possess adequate information and knowledge to supplement the view of the student.

As unfortunately, because the quality and accessibility of education varies so greatly between regions, the educational system of our country often fails to deliver the level of education necessary to ensure good competency. Many educational institutional have limited resources for buying books, stationary, furniture and other class room materials. Teachers also lack adequate qualification and training to engage their students in learning. Their lesson plans are most often outdated or irrelevant. Now, if the teacher's scope of gathering information and knowledge is limited how can you expect magic and wonders from teachers as well as students? These jeopardize the available quality of education.

But now, the pace of technological revolution and emergence of a knowledge society has changed the traditional role of teacher. In present scenario, teachers need to help their students in: how to learn, how to grow in future, how to develop study skills, how to conduct fundamental research, how to examine, evaluate and access information and also how to question and then dismantle unauthentic structure of knowledge and cognition if need be. Therefore, the problem stated as: "A study on integrating information and communication technology in teacher education".

Statement of the Problem

A present study is entitled "A Study on Integrating Information and Communication Technology in Teacher Education".

Operational Definition of Key Terms

Integration

Integration generally means combining parts so that they work together or form a whole.

ICT

Information and communication technology is defined, as the use of hardware and software for efficient management of information *i.e.,* storage, retrieval, processing, communication diffusion, and sharing of information for social, economical and cultural enlistment.

Teacher Education

According to Goods Dictionary of Education Teacher education means, all the formal and non-formal activities and experiences that help to qualify a person to assume responsibilities of a member of the educational profession or to discharge his responsibilities more effectively.

The investigator defined Teacher education means encompasses teaching skills, sound pedagogical theory and professional skills.

Objectives of the Study

The overall objective of the study is to picture the

1. To study the benefits of using ICT in education.
2. To find out the availability of ICT in teacher education.
3. To find out the knowledge and skills in developing and use of technology in education.
4. To study the variables in developing ICT in teacher education.

Hypothesis of the Study

1. There is no significant difference between the male and female teachers in the education development through ICT.
2. There is no significant difference between ICT knowledge and skills among the teachers with respect to their attended in service programme.
3. There is no significant difference between ICT knowledge and skills among the teachers with respect to their educational qualification.
4. There is a significant difference between in ICT knowledge and skills between rural and urban school teachers.
5. There is no highly significant difference between ICT knowledge and skills among the teachers with respect to their management of the school.

Method Selected for the Study

For the present study, the investigator employed the survey method. Survey method is a method for collecting and analyzing data obtained from large number of respondent representing a specific population collected through highly structured techniques.

Population

In this research the population consists of all higher secondary school teachers in Cuddalore District.

Sample

The investigator selected 150 samples have been collected from higher secondary school teachers in Cuddalore district, by using simple random sampling techniques.

Tool

Effectiveness of evaluation largely depends upon the accuracy of measurement. Accuracy of measurement in turn depends on the instrument. The tool is of many types. The investigator selected the questionnaire form. The tools had 45 items. The questionnaire prepared and developed by D. Sivakumar (2010) and it was used to collect the data in this study.

ICT Scale

ICT in Teacher Scale consists of 50 questions All the questions are 3 point scale carry 3, 2, 1 for positive responses and 1, 2, 3, mark for the responses in negative statements. There are 38 positive statements and 12 negative statements. (3,7,13,17,21,25,31,35,39,42,45 and 49 are negative statements, the remaining items are positive statements).

- *Reliability of the Tool:* To find out the reliability of the tool, test and retest method was used. The correlation value is 0.86.
- *Validity of the Tool:* In this investigation the tools were submitted to the panel of experts. They scrutinized the developed tools and their suggestions were incorporated. Thus the validity of the tools is established.

Collection of Data

With the permission of the heads of the Institutions of all selected schools. The instruction regarding the tool was clearly given. The teachers were properly motivated so as to enable them to participate sincere and to give real response. The investigator selected and received the information from the teachers as per distribution of the sample.

Statistical Techniques used

The following statistical techniques were used such as mean, standard deviation, 't' test and "F" test.

Hypothesis: 1

There is no significant difference between the male and female teachers in the education development through ICT.

Table 27.1: Test of Significant Difference in ICT Between Male and Female Teachers

Sex	N	Mean	S.D	't' value	Level of Significance
Male	76	74.24	11.61	1.260	Not significance
Female	74	71.32	13.18		

Table 27.1 shows that the computed value of 't' 1.260 is less than the critical value of 2.61 at 0.01 level and hence it is not significant. Consequently, the null hypothesis is to be accepted. And it can be said that there is no significant difference in ICT between male and female teachers.

Hypothesis: 2

There is no significant difference between ICT knowledge and skills among the teachers with respect to their attended in-service programme.

Table 27.2: Test of Significant Difference Between ICT Knowledge and Skills among the Teachers with Respect to their Attended in-service Programme

Responds	N	Mean	S.D	't' value	Level of Significance
Yes	87	73.10	11.38	0.635	Not significant
No	63	71.58	14.54		

Table 27.2 shows that the computed value of 't' 0.635 is less than the critical value of 2.61 at 0.01 level and hence it not significant. Consequently, the null hypothesis is to be accepted. And it can be said that there is no significant difference between ICT knowledge and skills among the teachers with respect to their attended in-service programme.

Hypothesis: 3

There is no significant difference between ICT knowledge among the teachers with respect to their educational qualification.

Table 27.3: Test of Significant Difference Between ICT Knowledge among the Teachers with Respect to their Educational Qualification

Sources of Variations	Sum of Squares	Mean Squares	F	Level Significant
Between the group	242.473	121.236	0.765	Not significant
with in the group	18553.119	158.574		

Table 27.3 shows that the computed value of 'F' 0.765 is less than the critical value of 4.75 at 0.01 level and hence it is not significant. Consequently, the null hypothesis is to be accepted. And it can be said that there is no significant difference between ICT knowledge among the teachers with respect to their educational qualification.

Hypothesis: 4

There is no significant difference in ICT knowledge and skills between rural and urban school teachers.

Table 27.4: Test of Significant Difference in ICT Knowledge and Skills Between Rural and Urban School Teachers

Locality	N	Mean	S.D	't' value	Level of Significant
Rural	66	70.15	12.98	2.79	Significant
Urban	84	76.58	10.83		

Table 27.4 shows that the computed value of 't' 2.79 is greater than the critical value of 2.61 at 0.01 levels and hence it is significant. Consequently, the null hypothesis is to be rejected. And it can be said that there is significant difference in ICT knowledge and skills between rural and urban school teachers.

Hypothesis: 5

There is no significant difference between ICT knowledge and skills among the teachers with respect to their management of the school.

Table 27.5: Test of Significance of Difference Between the Management of the School and Teacher's Knowledge and Skills About ICT

Sources of Variation	Sum of Squares	Mean Square	'F' value	Level of Significant
Between group	366.211	183.105	1.162	Not Significant
Within Group	18429.381	157.516		

Table 27.5 shows that the computed value of 'F' 1.162 is less than the critical value of 4.75 at 0.01 levels and hence it is not significant. Consequently, the null hypothesis is to be accepted.

Findings

- There is no significant difference between the male and female teachers in the education development through ICT.
- There is no significant difference between ICT knowledge and skills among the teachers with respect to their attended in service programme.
- There is no significant difference between ICT knowledge among the teachers with respect to their educational qualification.
- There is a significant difference between in ICT knowledge and skills between rurai and urban school teachers.
- There is no highly significant difference between ICT knowledge and skills among the teachers with respect to their management of the school.

Discussion

The result of the present study implied that there was adequate knowledge in ICT among teachers. There is a significant difference between in ICT knowledge and skills between rural and urban school teachers. Compare the mean score urban teachers have high then rural teachers. This is may be due to the fact that, internet facility and other technological facility are not available in rural areas. Internet facilities should be provided to the rural areas and computer literacy programme needs to be conducted in rural areas.

Conclusion

ICT opens a window into the world of technology. It will also open new avenue of employment, either self or external agency based. ICT plays a vital role in education. So today, teachers are using the technology in their subject and they want to improve their knowledge in ICT while teaching. Teaching methodology will shift from teacher-centered education to learner-centered education. Teacher's dominance will be replaced by the knowledge dominance. So the government should give more funds, for the establishment of ICT programme and more special in-services training programme has to be conducted, to give hand-on-training in operating technologies and other widely used application software to the teachers. Hence, in this way ICT can be profitably used in classroom teaching to make the teaching-learning process more effective. For that the teachers should have knowledge of the fundamental operation of a technology and widely used application software.

Suggestions for Further Study

- The present study has studied covers only at Cuddalore Districts. A similar study may also be conducted in other Districts of Tamil Nadu.
- A study on effectiveness of other latest technological features can be undertaken.
- A similar study may be undertaken for all the college levels.
- Similar studies can be carried out among other levels of teachers working in universities, colleges, high schools and primary schools.
- This study may be extended to a large sample taking some more variables.

REFERENCES

Anjali Pahad and Avani Maniar, (1997). Integrating ICT in Teacher Education. A Case Study National Conference On Technology *vs.* Teacher, Indian Council for Research in Educational Media Bharathidasan University, Tiruchirappalli - 620 023.

D. R. Goel Chhaya Goel, Malhar F. Earnest, (1997). ICT in Education: Changes and Challenges, CASE Faculty of Education M.S. University of Baroda.

John W. Best and James. V. Khan (1995). Research in Education, Prentice Hall of India Private Ltd. New Delhi.

Kothari, C. R. (1994). Research Methodology and Techniques, Willey Eastern Limited, New Delhi.

Kumar, K. L., (1997). Educational Technology, New Age International Publishers, New Delhi.

Mangal, S. K., (2004). Fundamentals of Educational Technology, Ludhiana, Prakash Brother Educational Publishers.

Palaniappan, V. P., (1998). Computer and Educational Technology, December 98 Sona printers, New Delhi.

Peter Hosie and Renato Schibeci., (2005). Checklist and Context-bound Evaluations Technology, Vol. 36, No. 5, p. 881.

Purushothaman, (1997), Integrating Technology in Teacher Education Programme National Conference on Technology *vs.* Teacher, Indian Council for Research in Educational Media Bharathidasan University, Tiruchirappalli - 620 023.

Sankhala. D. P., (2007). Educational Technology Adhyayan Publisers and Distributor, New Delhi.

Sharma, R. A., Educational Technology and Management, (2004) R. Lall Book Depot, Near Government, Inter College, Meerut (U.P).

Page 202-208

Recent Trend in Educational Research
Edited by: **Dr. D. Sivakumar**
Edition: **2015**
ISBN: 978-93-5056-741-8
Published by: **Discovery Publishing House Pvt. Ltd., New Delhi (India)**

28

Perspective and Issues in Higher Education

Nagashree. S. N.

INTRODUCTION

Indian universities offer various subjects at degree level. These pertain to basic science like: physics, Chemistry, Biology; social science like: Economics, Sociology, Psychology. These also form as the basic analysis of the subject under study from where a student can branch out in the area of interest which may lead to process of research and specialization. There by creating newer theories and improvement in the art of living.

The present scenario for the above mentioned subject and others have been on the downward trend. The courses offered in basic Science and Social science have failed to attract students to take them up. Just for the sake of getting a bachelors degree students are enrolling in social science courses. Study of certain basic science courses have been closed down because of lack of students.

The difficulty is that it is subject oriented than the leaner orientation where combination of courses offered in fixed and a student may have to take the subject unwillingly. Once the

Department of Economics, Govt. Pre-University College, Kolar.

given combination is taken students cannot revert to other subjects. The studying of inter-disciplinary subject is also not allowed. Each subjects in dependent on another for its existence. There is lack of development in inter disciplinary subjects. Subjects which ought to get importance leading to inter disciplinary research are not permitted this makes one arrive at a dead end. A student finds it hard to understand a subject in totality if inter disciplinary subjects are not given importance.

The emerging areas of Nano-Technology, a symbiosis of Biology and Chemistry in needed for development of effective drugs for treatment; infant stage of physiological psychology, lack of awareness about socio-economic surveys have never been given due emphasis. A Teacher is restricted to a particular subject through specialized as master degree holds and a Ph.D. Degree awarded. For the good understanding of subjects' interdisciplinary approach in needed.

Basic and Social Science at Degree Level

The current scenario can be analyzed at three phases: *(i)* Student Level, *(ii)* Teachers Level and *(iii)* Government Policy.

Student's Level

The courses offered are basic Degree, needed for specialization and research. The student who enrolls always looks at the job prospects if the course taken today will fetch him a job and comforts of life. As IT and BT courses offering campus recruitment has made engineering courses more incrative than basic Sciences.

Table 28.1: Number of Teachers in Institute of Higher Education

Institution	Enrolment in '000	Teacher in '000	Student-Teacher Ratio
University Departments and University Colleges	13,88	77	18
Affiliated	90,93	395	23
Total	104,81	472	22

Source: UGC Annual Report

The bachelors Degree like: engineering, medical and commerce have been made lucrative by which a student would opt for that course. Here the basic science and social science has failed to take students because lack of incentive, campus recruitment, attractive salaries to lead comfortable life. It's quite natural that the pivot shifts is towards better standard of living.

Teacher's Level

At teacher level it lacks professionalism most of the 2nd generation teachers have retired and the recruitment policy of the government has been on a decline. The remuneration to the teachers is low when compared to other profession. This makes students taken up other jobs in different fields. The teaching aids in the colleges are backward. It is still in stage of chalk and talk. No other techniques are employed. Teaching methods have been learning through rutting and reproducing the same in order to score marks.

The Syballus set for Indian Universities are low when compared to other foreign Universities the application of the subject in practical would in restrict. There is lack of interest in teachers to teach and inspire. Teachers should know a little about inter-related subject subjects so as to make teaching effective. A Teacher has to keep updated with the subject in order to answer the questions raised by students. The introduction of semester has not made any effective changes.

The assignment system has been nothing but copying from a prescribed text-book. There are hardly any project, been done. So the motive with which the internal assessment has been introduced has failed to instigate research at Degree Level. The student-Teacher enrollment has been high due to which individual attention and inspiring them to take up research as their career has failed. Awareness about entrance exam to get into Research institute is not given by the teachers.

Table 28.2: Graduate and PG Output

Faculty/Course	Graduate	PG
Arts, B.A.	972720	306419
Science, B.Sc	327775	74295
Commerce, B.Com	373192	94426

Source: Selected Educational Statistics (SES) based on UGC Report

Effective teaching methods have to be adopted depending on the student. Teachers follow the same method over the years. The rural and urban disparity is evident. Teachers also lack communicative skill and interaction with students is less.

Government Policy Level

Education is a state subject and its policy will affect the education pattern in a state. The skill formation about qualitative aspect is directly dependent on education policy. The policy in the state emphasizes on Universalization of primary and secondary education a little importance given to basic and social Science at higher level of education. There is more number of engineering colleges which are manufacturing students than acquired. Certain branches in engineering are neglected. Apart from them the colleges offering basic and Social Science lack infrastructure, lab, quality teaching.

Table 28.3: Distribution of Central and State Universities

Type	Number
General	126
Agriculture	35
Technology	14
Language	11
Medical	9
Law	6
Women	5

Source: UGC Annual Report

If proper incentive, recruitment and improvement in teaching quality are not done then it's sure that courses at basic and social Science have to be closed down.

Basic and Social Science at Research Level

Students who take up Degree courses like B.A. B.SC are either that who cannot afford other courses or who takes up for the sake of getting Degree. Motivating them is a difficult task but one should identify their potentiality in a subject or inter related aspects at Degree level by conducting, Workshop, Symposium, Seminar, discussion about latest innovations at various subjects. It should be student oriented to motivate them.

The teachers should also counsel such students in initial stage when they take up such basic courses and motivate them to take up research. This motivation in lacking from teachers side as they themselves haven't taken up research work. Research up to doctoral level is seen end people who reach that stage in few in number. Faculty improvement programme [FIP] is granted but we hardly see qualitative improvement. Once a person achieve doctoral Degree that person is not interested in post doctoral research.

Table 28.4: Enrolment by Levels and Major Discipline

Year	General Graduate Arts, Commerce and Science	PG	PhD.
1980-1981	1886428	291341	25417
1990-1991	3285776	354216	32468
2000-2001	7244915	647338	45004
2001-2002	7139497	647016	53119
2002-2003	7633125	782590	65357
2003-2004	8026147	806636	65525

Source: Statistical Educational Statistics, Different Years

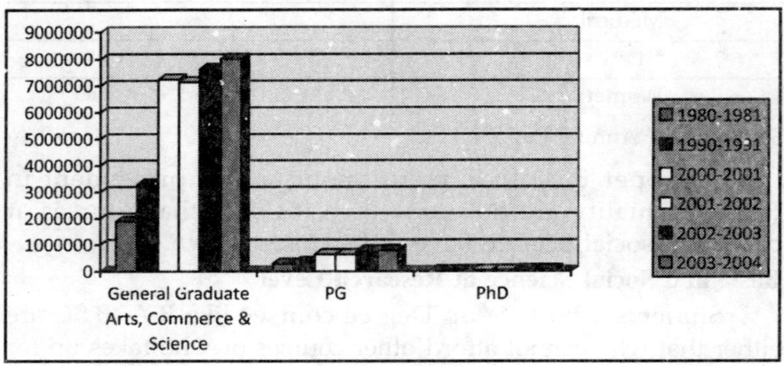

Fig. 28.1:

Research in not an overnight phenomenon but it's a continuous process. One needs Government support for research and proper identification of that research. Expenditure on R and D of GDP in 1996-2003 was 0.81, low when compared to other countries. Research should also include inter-country-University research collaboration to improve area of research. Resources allocation for research in meager and country's foreign policy still relies on the import of technology, personnel and material. Lack of incentive to researchers also puts off and desire to pursue career in research. If a researcher wants anything in an inter-disciplinary area it is almost impossible. At research, if, grant given to aided staff they prolong to take grant and not work. In the mean while research document produced is not of good quality.

Table 28.5: Gross Enrolment Ratio (GER) in Higher Education by Region

Countries	GER
Countries in Transition	36.5
Developed Countries	54.6
Developing Countries	11.3
World	23.2
India Tentative	**About 10%**

Source: Higher Education in World, the Financing of University. (Palgrave Macmillan)

Faulty education policy does not promote research attitude. It needs more resources to be mobilized for developing techniques. Government does not have resource for research and development because they need quick returns for improvements which do not happen in research in basic and Social Science. Those research documents which are qualitative and can be adopted by Government are not implemented because of lack of resources.

Suggestion for Improvement

1. Right resource person for orientation programme for teachers.
2. More documentary made to make teaching method easy through LCD'S and OHP'S.
3. Project and assignment should give practical experience leading to application of it at work Place.

4. Leadership quality, communication skill, would motivate students to take up careers in research.
5. Research oriented syllabus.
6. Teacher and student ratio should be low to explore the researching ability of a student.
7. Courses offered should be learner oriented. Students should be offered subjects which Interest them.
8. Government should allocate more resources:
   (i) recruitment of teachers should be done as the number of persons taking up the profession depleting;
   (ii) lack of proper incentive when compared to other areas. Teaching profession has to be made on par with others;
   (iii) more resource towards researching areas. Participation of private should be encouraged in R and D.

Conclusion

At Student level, leaner oriented course, practical oriented syllabus should motivate students for taking up a basic and social Science. At teachers level more attractive salaries and incentives should make more people take up profession. This should lead to more research oriented works. At Government level they have to mobilize resource to employ more people to improve the art of living. The projection of people taking social and basic science is bleak. A national educational policy should be made to mobilize resource that basic and social science at degree level and research have to be given top priority. The quality should also be ensured through various commissions.

Page 209-223
Recent Trend in Educational Research
Edited by: **Dr. D. Sivakumar**
Edition: **2015**
ISBN: 978-93-5056-741-8
Published by: **Discovery Publishing House Pvt. Ltd., New Delhi (India)**

29

Relational Studies on Home Environment and Emotional Maturity of Higher Secondary School Students

Anand Babu

INTRODUCTION

One of the dimensions of personal experience is the emotional or affective dimension. Emotional process is not an isolated phenomenon but a component of general experience, constantly influencing and influenced by other process going on at the same time.

The home is basically a unit in which parents and children live together. Its key position rests on its multiple functions in relation to overall development of its members, their protection and overall well being. The home is the oldest and the most important of all the institutions that man has devised to regulate and integrate his behaviour as he strives to satisfy his basis needs. Home is influencing the individual in modifying the social behaviour. It is essential for a healthy living, the best home environment, irrespective of the age of the individual.

In higher secondary school students, the home-environment plays a major role towards moulding the personality of an adolescent into a man or woman. Home is

Assistant Professor, St. Johns College of Education, Palayamkottai.

orienting the individual in the social skills like developing social attitudes, cooperating with other social like, developing social attitudes, cooperating with other social members, learns to accept the feeiing of others, acquires the skills of recognizing others irrespective of their Gender, standard and so on. Emotional maturity is the process of impulse control through the agency of self. It is a process of readjustment, which is patterned in accordance with the approved expression and repression in their cultures.

Need for the Present Study

Each and every student must understand the home conditions and problems. They should realize the necessity of maintaining the environment. Education is the best outcome in the environment in which they live. Students need good home environment. Home is the first institution. The home is basically a unit in which parents and children live together. Family's first position depends on the multiple responsibilities and functions of each and every member of the home to develop protection and care of the members.

The home - environment is caused by various factors like type of family, size of family, marital status of the family, socio-economic background of the home and so on. In such a situation an individual has to come up with the social desirable dimension of behaviour. In this context this is inevitable to study the relationship between home environment and Emotional Maturity among higher secondary students. Emotions are strong mental states involving excitement which give rise to feeling and passions. They play an important role in life and contribute in the personal and social adjustment of the individual. Usually emotions give us energy to face particular situation in life and the work as conditions disturb our mental equilibrium and reasoning. They serve as media of communication between individuals and guide the individual since emotions are frequent, they are all temporary. The person who is apparently matured and balanced in his emotional life suddenly becomes upset, restoring to temperamental outbursts. Hence emotional maturity plays a vital role in their individuals' personality.

Statement of the Problem

The problem entitled as: "Relational Studies on Home Environment and Emotional Maturity of Higher Secondary School Students".

Operational Key Terms and Definitions

The terms used in the present study are as follows.

Home Environment

Home environment is the social and environmental characteristics of families. Home environment involves the circumstances and social climate conditions within families. Home environment is defined as the social setting in which the child interacts with the members of the family.

Emotional Maturity

Emotional actually is "A Process or readjustment, the infancy learns under parental supervision what situations after permissible opportunities for emotional reactions and to what extent, so that primitive elemental psychological response that we call 'emotion' becomes patterned in accordance with the approved from the emotional maturity is the process of impulse control through the agency of 'self'. It is a process of readjustment, which is patterned. In accordance with the approved express and repression in their cultures.

Higher Secondary Students

By higher secondary students the Investigator means the students doing standards XI and XII Standard higher secondary schools in Tamil Nadu state.

Objectives of the Study

1. To find out the level of home environment of higher secondary students is high.
2. To find out level of home environment among boys and girls students is high.
3. To find out whether there is any significance difference between boys and girls higher secondary students with respect to their home environment.
4. To find out whether there is any significance difference between XI and XII Standard higher secondary students with respect to their home environment.

5. To find out whether there is any significance difference between rural and urban higher secondary students with respect to their home environment.
6. To find out the emotional maturity of higher secondary students is high.
7. To find out level of emotional maturity among boys and girls students is high.
8. To find out whether there is any significance difference between boys and girls higher secondary students with respect to their emotional maturity.
9. To find out whether there is any significance difference between XI and XII standard higher secondary students with respect to their emotional maturity.
10. To find out whether there is any significance difference between rural and urban higher secondary students with respect to their emotional maturity.
11. To find out whether there is any relationship between home environment and emotional maturity of higher secondary students with respect to background variables.

Hypotheses of the Study

1. There is no significant difference between boys and girls higher secondary students with respect to their home environment.
2. There is no significant difference between XI and XII standard higher secondary students with respect to their home environment.
3. There is no significant difference between rural and urban higher secondary students with respect to their home environment.
4. There is no significant difference between boys and girls higher secondary students with respect to their emotional maturity.
5. There is no significant difference between XI and XII standard higher secondary students with respect to their emotional maturity.
6. There is no significant difference between rural and urban school higher secondary students with respect to their emotional maturity.

7. There is no significant relationship between Home Environmental and Emotional Maturity with reference to background variables.

Method used for the Present Study

The investigator has adopted the survey method of research to find out the Relational Studies on Home Environment and Emotional Maturity of higher secondary Students. According to William Wiersma (1986) "Survey research deals with incidents, distribution and relationship of educational, psychological and sociological variables".

The Sample

The study was conducted in Thoothukudi districts only. In Thoothukudi district, there are 109 higher secondary schools functioning under the state board syllabus. Of the above schools 33 are government higher secondary school 71 are management aided higher secondary schools and 5 are management unaided higher secondary schools, the investigator has selected 6 higher secondary schools. The investigator has used stratified random sampling technique to select a sample of 300 students (137 Males and 163 Females).

Tools used

The following tools have been used to collect data. *(i)* Home Environment Scale, *(ii)* Emotional Maturity Scale

1. *Home Environment Scale*: Home Environment Scale was standardized by D. Sivakumar (2008) was used for assessing the home environment of the higher secondary students.

Validity and Reliability

The author of the tool established validity of the tool. To ascertain the validity of the tool. The tool was given to a panel of experts consisting of 5 eminent scholars of the different colleges each expert was asked to indicate the degree to which each item assessed the home environment of the respondents. The degree of agreement of experts on each item indicated the validity of the tool corrections were made in the items of the tool in accordance with their suggestions. According to their views, the tool possesses satisfactory content validity. Reliability is the degree of accuracy and consistency. The prepared tool was subjected to test-retest method. The responses of the respondents were scored and the correlation co-efficient was found to be 0.85 for the two sets of scores.

Scoring Procedure

The respondents were instructed to choose their degree of agreement to the statement by putting a tick mark (√) against the space provided. The score may vary from 5-1 all items are positive statements.

2. *Emotional Maturity Scale*: Emotional maturity scale constructed and validated by the investigator.

Description of the Draft Tool

A research tool plays a major role in any worthwhile research as it is the sole factor in determining the sound data and in arriving at a perfect conclusion for about the problem. In the present investigation in order to measure the emotional maturity among higher secondary students the investigator has used the open type questionnaire. The researcher referred various books, magazines, websites and journals pertaining to emotional maturity to have clarity of concepts. The investigator had discussed with educational experts and collected information and ideas about the content for the development of the tool. The tool had consisted five dimensions of forty five questions each questions in the three point scales. The author established reliability and validity of the tool.

Table 29.1: Level of Home Environment among Higher Secondary Students

Variables	Low		Average		High	
	No	%	No	%	No	%
Home environment	68	22.7	163	54.3	69	23.0

It is inferred from Table 29.1 that 22.7 per cent of the students have low, 54.3 per cent of them have moderate and 23.0 per cent of them have high level of home Environment.

It is inferred from Table 29.2 that 24.0 per cent of the male students have low, 57.2 per cent of them have moderate and 18.8 per cent of them have high level of home environment, among 19.6 per cent of the female students have low, 47.8 per cent of them have moderate and 32.6 per cent of them have high level of home environment.

Table 29.2: Level of Home Environment among Higher Secondary Students with Reference to Gender

Dimensions	Variable	Low		Average		High	
		No	%	No	%	No	%
Home environment	Boys	27	24.0	90	57.2	20	18.8
	Girls	30	19.6	104	47.8	29	32.6

Null Hypothesis 1

There is no significance difference between boys and girls students with respect to their home environment.

Table 29.3: The Significance of the Difference between the Mean of the Home Environment of Boys and Girls Students

Gender	N	Mean	S.D.	't' value	Level of Significance
Male	137	42.22	12.79	2.64	significant
Female	163	46.17	13.00		

(At 5% level of significance, the table value of 't' is 1.96)

It is inferred from Table 29.3 that computed 't' value is found to be 2.64 which is significance at 0.05 level. Hence the null hypothesis is rejected. It is inferred that boys and girls has significantly differentiate the higher secondary students with respect to their home environment.

Null Hypothesis 2

There is no significance difference between the XI and XII standard students with respect to their home environment.

Table 29.4: The Significance of the Difference between the Mean of the Home Environment of XI Standard and XII Standard Students

Standard	N	Mean	S.D.	't' value	Level of Significance
XI Standard	155	45.02	12.42	0.79	Not Significant
XII Standard	145	46.20	13.24		

(At 5% level of significance, the table value of 't' is 1.96)

It is inferred from Table 29.4 that computed 't' value is found to be 0.79 which is not significance at 0.05 level. Hence the null hypothesis is accepted. It is inferred that XI Standard and XII Standard has no significantly differentiate the higher secondary students with respect to their home environment.

Null Hypothesis 3

There is no significance difference between the rural and urban higher secondary students with respect to their home environment.

Table 29.5: Difference between the Rural and Urban Higher Secondary Students with Respect to their Home Environment

Nativity of the Student	N	Mean	S.D.	't' value	Level of Significance
Rural	159	46.25	12.90	2.19	significant
Urban	141	42.85	13.85		

(At 5% level of significance, the table value of 't' is 1.96)

It is inferred from Table 29.5 that computed 't' value is found to be 2.19 which is significance at 0.05 level. Hence the null hypothesis is rejected. It is inferred that the rural and urban students has significant difference between the higher secondary students with respect to their home environment.

Table 29.6: Level of Emotional Maturity among Higher Secondary Students

Dimensions	Low		Average		High	
	No	%	No	%	No	%
Emotional Unstability	50	16.7	209	69.7	41	13.6
Emotional Regression	55	18.3	205	648.	40	13.3
Social Adjustment	59	19.7	199	66.3	42	14.0
Personality Disintegration	62	20.7	191	63.7	47	15.6
Lack of Independence	63	21.0	196	65.3	41	13.7
Total Emotional Maturity	62	20.7	196	65.3	42	14.0

The Level is Average

It is inferred from Table 29.6 that 20.7 of the students have low, 65.3 per cent of them have moderate and 14.0 per cent of them have high level of Emotional Maturity.

Table 29.7: Level of Emotional Maturity of Higher Secondary Students with Reference to Gender

Dimensions	Sex	Low		Average		High	
		No	%	No	%	No	%
Emotional Unstability	Male	23	17.3	98	70	16	12.7
	Female	28	16.0	113	70.7	22	13.3
Emotional Regression	Male	20	17.4	99	69.3	18	13.3
	Female	30	20.7	108	65.3	25	14.0
Social Adjustment	Male	21	16.7	97	70.7	19	12.6
	Female	27	18.0	110	64.7	26	17.3
Personality Disintegration	Male	22	21.3	97	66.7	18	12.0
	Female	28	18.7	105	64	30	17.3
Lack of Independence	Male	30	22.7	90	64.7	17	12.6
	Female	34	20.7	103	62.0	26	17.3
Total Emotional Maturity	Male	30	22.0	89	66.0	18	12.0
	Female	34	18.7	101	64.7	28	16.6

The Level is Average

Table 29.7 reveals that 22.0 per cent of the male students have low, 66.0 per cent of them have moderate and 12.0 per cent of them have high level of emotional maturity, among 18.7 per cent of the female students have low, 64.7 per cent of them have moderate and 16.6 per cent of them have high level of emotional maturity.

Null Hypothesis 4

There is no significant difference between male and female students in their emotional maturity and its dimensions.

Since the calculated 't' value is greater than the table value of 't' at 5 per cent level of significance, there is significant difference between male and female students in emotional maturity and its dimensions emotional regression, social adjustment, personality disintegration and lack of independence. But, there is no significant difference in emotional unstability, as the calculated 't' value is less than the table value of 't' at 5 per cent level of significance.

Table 29.8: Difference between Male and Female Students in their Emotional Maturity and its Dimensions

Dimensions	Male (N=137)		Female (N=163)		Calculated 't' value	Remarks at 5% Level
	Mean	S.D	Mean	S.D		
Emotional Unstability	26.04	7.88	26.17	8.25	0.14	NS
Emotional Regression	25.06	7.94	22.43	7.14	3.01	S
Social Adjustment	25.99	7.93	22.63	6.59	3.99	S
Personality Disintegration	24.43	8.92	20.42	7.50	4.22	S
Lack of Independence	21.63	7.17	20.07	6.29	2.00	S
Total Emotional Maturity	123.16	33.82	111.51	29.05	3.20	S

(At 5% level of significance, the table value of 't' is 1.97)

Null Hypothesis 5

There is no significant difference between XI standard and XII standard students in their emotional maturity and its dimensions.

Table 29.9: Difference between XI Standard and XII Standard Students in their Emotional Maturity and its Dimensions

Dimensions	XI Standard (N=155)		XII Standard (N=145)		Calculated 't' value	Remarks at 5% Level
	Mean	S.D	Mean	S.D		
Emotional Unstability	26.59	8.24	25.62	7.87	1.04	NS
Emotional Regression	23.83	7.48	23.67	7.84	0.18	NS
Social Adjustment	24.54	7.98	24.09	6.94	0.53	NS
Personality Disintegration	23.30	8.81	21.55	8.05	1.79	NS
Lack of Independence	20.78	7.13	20.93	6.42	0.19	NS
Total Emotional Maturity	119.03	33.46	115.63	30.50	0.92	NS

(At 5% level of significance, the table value of 't' is 1.97)

Since the calculated 't' value is less than the table value of 't' at 5 per cent level of significance, there is no significant difference between XI and XII Standard students in emotional maturity and its dimensions emotional unstability, emotional regression, social adjustment, personality disintegration and lack of independence.

Null Hypothesis 6

There is no significant difference between Rural and Urban students in their emotional maturity and its dimensions.

Table 29.10: Difference between Rural and Urban Students in their Emotional Maturity

Dimensions	Rural (N=155)		Urban (N=145)		Calcul-ated 't' value	Remarks at 5% Level
	Mean	S.D	Mean	S.D		
Emotional Unstability	25.70	7.81	31	9.39	2.63	S
Emotional Regression	23.49	7.64	26.83	7.25	2.11	S
Social Adjustment	24.17	7.54	26.09	6.50	1.34	NS
Personality Disintegration	22.12	8.23	26.13	10.41	1.80	NS
Lack of Independence	20.56	6.72	24.35	6.65	2.62	S
Total Emotional Maturity	115.92	31.38	134.39	35.16	2.44	S

(At 5% level of significance, the table value of 't' is 1.97)

Since the calculated 't' value is greater than the table value of 't' at 5 per cent level of significance, there is significant difference between Rural and Urban students in emotional maturity and its dimensions emotional unstability, emotional regression, and lack of independence. But, there is no significant difference in social adjustment and personality disintegration, as the calculated 't' value is less than the table value of 't' at 5 per cent level of significance.

Hypothesis 7

There is no significant relationship between Home Environmental and Emotional Maturity with reference to background variables.

Since the calculated value of 'r' is greater than the table value at 5 per cent level of significance, the hypothesis is rejected. Therefore there is significant relationship between home environmental and emotional maturity with reference to background variables.

Table 29.11: Relationship between Home Environment and Emotional Maturity with Reference to Background Variables

S. No.	Variables	Categories	"r" value	Table value	Result
1.	Sex	Male	0.238	0.139	S
		Female	0.159	0.139	S
2.	Standard	XI standard	0.248	0.139	S
		XII standard	0.225	0.139	S
3.	Locality of the school	Rural	0.196	0.139	S
		Urban	0.141	0.139	S

Findings

- The level of home environment of higher secondary students is average.
- The level of home environment of higher secondary students with reference to sex is average. Among the average value, boys higher secondary students have high score (57.2%). The level of girls higher secondary students in home environment is low (47.8%).
- There is a significance difference between boys and girls students with respect to their home environment.
- There is no significance difference between the XI and XII standard students with respect to their home environment.
- There is significant difference between rural and urban higher secondary students with respect to their home environment.
- The level of emotional maturity of higher secondary students is average.
- The level of emotional maturity of higher secondary students with reference to sex is average. Among the average value, boys higher secondary students have high score (66.0%). The level of girls' higher secondary students in emotional maturity is low (64.7%).
- There is no significant difference between boys and girls higher secondary students in their emotional unstability. But there is significant difference between boys and girls

students in their emotional regression, social adjustment, personality disintegration, lack of independence and total emotional maturity.

- There is no significant difference between XI and XII standard higher secondary students with respect to their emotional maturity and its dimensions.

Recommendations

Based on the findings, the investigator would like to present the following recommendations.

- Parents should provide congenial atmosphere for the student to study well at home.
- Hence, female students should be given more chances to mingle with the society.
- Students belonging to low income must be equally treated as other students.
- Girls and co-education school students may be trained up to know 'What I am?' and 'What can I do?'
- Generally special programmes such as interaction with others, educational tour, to play with others, participation of debates, conversations and competitions may be conducted among the students to get ideas, perceptions and values that characterize 'I' or 'me' and every one should recognize by themselves about various aspects.
- Teacher should encourage feelings of cohesiveness among students through effective communication. This beneficial cohesive feeling can be induced by arranging tours and trips and by taking them to the places where people are in need of external help. Students can be taken to various sports where natural calamities cause dander to common public and can be made to help those sufferers. This sort of experience will give sense of sensitivity and their knowledge to recognize their home environment.
- Alternative types of work while studying should not be given by their family members.
- The financial situation of the students has a negative impact on the students' academic achievements. Poor

performance may be due to the fact that their needs are not satisfied. These types of children could be financial aided by way of scholarship, loans and concessions, which could serve as motivating factor to do better in their studies.

Suggestions for Further Research

- Replica of the present study should be undertaken with college students.
- The emotional maturity along with other psychological variables recommended for probing.
- The same study should be undertaken in other parts of our country.
- The variables of the study like demographic variables should be considered.
- A study on the psycho-socio correlates of the emotional maturity of the adolescents can be conducted.
- The present study can be extended in terms of population and sample.
- An investigation into the emotional maturity of the adolescents in relation to their school environment can be conducted.
- A study on the emotional maturity of the high school students in relation of their self-concept can be conducted.
- A comparative study of the emotional maturity of the matriculation and non-matriculation students can be arranged.

Conclusion

Higher secondary education plays a very significant role in every individual life since after this education all decisions are made for the future. Chronologically and psychologically, home starts the child off into life and its experiences. It is the original and basic source of informal and incidental learning which sale sequentially limits and slants the individuals' quality and rate of progress on different chosen fronts the overall influence of home itself through affection, care and attention which are diffused and displayed in different ways, on an appropriate scale of frequency and intensity. The present investigation clearly shows the stability of Emotional Maturity of the higher secondary students in different dimensions along with varied demographic variables. This may be due to the factors of both internal and external disturbances in the behaviour of the students. This necessitates proper guidance and counseling by teachers, parents, educationists and administrators.

REFERENCES

Agarwal, P. (2007). *"Modern Educational Research"*, Dominant Publishers and Distributors, New Delhi.

Amutha Ranjini, G. and Sivakumar, D. (2007). Classroom Environment and Academic Achievement in Biology of XI Standard in Thoothukudi District in Unpublished M.Ed Dissertation, Manonmanium Sundaranar University, Tirunelveli.

Arati, C. and Rathna Prabha C. (2004). Influence of family Environment on Emotion Competence of Adolescents", *Journal of Community Guidancee and Research*. Vol. 21, No. 2, 2004, pp. 215-17.

Basantia M. Jaga and Mukhopadhyaya D. (2001). "Effect of Environmental Factors on Achievement", *Educational Review*, Vol. 44, No. 11, November, 2001, p. 201.

Catteli, R. B. (1984). Handbook of Multivariate Experimental Psychology, Illinais; Dryden Press, Chaplin, *J. P. Dictionary of Psychology*, New York; Dell Publishing, Co.

Chauhan, S. S (2000). *"Advanced Educational Psychology"*. Vikas Publishing House Pvt. Ltd. New Delhi.

Keetz Mary A (1929). Social Position and Home Correlation of Habits, *Journal of Psychological Researcher*, Vol. 23.

Kiewra Kenneth. A; Dubais, (1991). Nelson, F, Christian David, Mcshare, Anne, Note taking Functions and Techniques *Journal of Educational Psychology* (June), Vol. 83 (2), pp. 240-245.

Amruth G. Kumar (2005). "Emotional Balance of Secondary School Students in Relation to their Home Environment", *Edutracks*, Vol. 4, No. 7, March 2005, pp. 31-32.

Thomas: Kellagam (1977). "Relationships between home Environment and Scholastic Behaviour in a Disadvantage Population" *Journal of Educational Psychology*, 60, 6, pp. 754-760.

Page 224-232
Recent Trend in Educational Research
Edited by: **Dr. D. Sivakumar**
Edition: **2015**
ISBN: 978-93-5056-741-8
Published by: **Discovery Publishing House Pvt. Ltd., New Delhi (India)**

30

Rashtriya Uchchatar Shiksha Abhiyan (RUSA)

A Boon for Higher Education

K. Thiyagu

INTRODUCTION

Rashtriya Uchchatar Shiksha Abhiyan (RUSA) is a centrally sponsored scheme proposed by the Ministry of Human Resources Development/UGC to ensure holistic planning at the state level and enhancement of allocations for the state institutions, which will spread over the next five-year two plan periods (XII and XIII Five-year Plans) and it will focus on state higher educational institutions. A sum of Rs. 5,00,00,000 has been earmarked for the implementation of RUSA in India during the XII and XIII Five-year Plan periods. Through RUSA it aims to cover 316 states public universities and 13,024 colleges across the country. The government is looking at brining various reforms to improve the quality of higher education sector by creation of a State Higher Education Council, creation of accreditation agencies, preparation of the state perspective plans, commitment of certain stipulated share of funds towards RUSA, academic, sectoral and institutional governance reforms, filling faculty positions etc. The funding will be provided in the

Assistant Professor in Mathematics, Dr. Sivanthi Aditanar College of Education, Tiruchendur - 628 215, Tamil Nadu.

(Centre: State) ratio of 90:10 for North-East States. The draft proposal of RUSA was approved by the Hon'ble Minister of Human Resource Development Government of India.

As per the RUSA document, greater emphasis will be laid on the improvement of the quality of teaching-learning processes in order to produce employable and competitive graduates, post-graduates and PhDs. With respect to the planning and funding approach, some key changes are envisaged; *(a)* funding will be more impact and result oriented; *(b)* various equity related schemes will be integrated for a higher impact; *(c)* instead of unplanned expansion, there will be a focus on consolidating and developing the existing system adding capacities; and *(d)* there will be a greater focus on research and innovation.

The RUSA emphasizes to promote reforms in the State Higher Education System by creating a facilitating institutional structure for planning and monitoring at the state level. It will help to promote autonomy in state universities and include governance in the institutions. One of the goals of RUSA will be to ensure academic examination reforms in the higher education institutions and enable conversion of some of the universities into research universities at par with the best in the world.

India is aiming at increasing the number of students in higher education and the Gross Enrolment Ratio (GER) from 18 per cent to 30 per cent over the next seven years. The HRD ministry presented their plans to the Consultative Committee where the Rashtriya Uchchatar Shiksha Abhiyan will take the Gross Enrolment Ratio (GER) from 18 per cent to 30 per cent. Estimated to cost Rs. 99,000 crores the scheme will envelop all other existing schemes. The crux of the scheme is in the central funding that will now go through the State Council of Higher Education instead of directly from the Centre and UGC to educational institutions. The funding will increase up to 90 per cent. It will be available to private institutions as will though based on certain norms and conditions.

Reforms in the State Higher Education System will be focused upon. A facilitating institutional structure for planning and monitoring at the state level will be created for this purpose. Autonomy in state universities and governance in the institutions will be promoted by this structure. RUSA will also aspire to bring about academic examination reforms in the higher education institutions. It will enable the upgrading of some universities into world class research universities. The MHRD will implement the scheme as a centrally sponsored scheme. Matching contribution from the state governments and union territories will be made. Eligibility criteria will be created for states in order to achieve meaningful impact through observation and appraisal. The institutions will however be monitoring themselves. The state government and the Centre will annually monitor the institutions through the Project Appraisal Board. The programme will also set up new universities and promote existing autonomous colleges to universities. It will also alter colleges to cluster universities with new model colleges. Existing degree colleges will be made into Model Colleges.

RUSA: A Tool for Improve Quality of Higher Education

The central government has come up with a new Scheme 'Rashtriya Uchchatar Shiksha Abhiyan' (RUSA) to improve quality in higher education and enhance Gross Enrolment Ratio (GER). The scheme is designed where the central government offers financial support to state governments to augment capacity on a revenue sharing basis formula of 65:35 between Centre and State government. This is an excellent idea to take forward. Gross Enrolment Ratio in higher education is the indicator which measures the percentage of eligible population which has access to higher education in age group between 18-23 years.

Rashtriya Uchchatar Shiksha Abhiyan scheme warrants state government to set up State Council for higher education and supporting agencies such as accrediting agency to assess and to monitor the quality of higher education in the state in line with National Assessment and Accreditation Council (NAAC).

One of the major reasons for falling quality in state educational institutions is the large scale appointment of teachers on ad-hoc basis such as contract basis and lecture hour basis. The new scheme mandates state governments to fill all vacant these posts for quality enhancement. This should be supplemented by reforms in institutional governance, administration, sectorial reforms, transparent administration, and setting of management information system to avail the benefits of the proposed scheme.

State Council for Higher Education is the statutory body comprises of 20 to 25 eminent academicians or public intellectuals with proven leadership qualities who will provide critical inputs for the overall development of the sector. It will plan, coordinate, monitor and evaluate higher education in the state and will be responsible for the maximum utilisation of resources by colleges and university under the scheme.

The implementation of the scheme will be spread over 12th and 13th five-year plan period and the funding to states will be on the basis of 'critical appraisal' of their plans for higher education, which includes strategy to address issues of equity, access and excellence in higher education. The continuity of the scheme depends on the performance outcome on the above parameters.

Goa government should take advantage of this scheme to improve quality in higher education in the state. It also provides employment opportunities to large number of educated unemployed youth. Academic fraternity should deliberate on this scheme seriously and all stakeholders should be consulted to implement the scheme for the benefit of the state.

Funding Pattern of RUSA

UGC is also not allowed to channelize funds through the state government or through any entity other than an educational institution, which makes it impossible for the UGC to fund any planning, and expansion activity through a state level higher education body. UGC as a regulator should be actively involved in planning for new institutions but the present system does not permit it to do so. Thus states often complain of being unaware of the development funds that come to the state institutions from the centre; this makes planning and funding very difficult for the states.

Under RUSA the centre aims at an 'optimum' solution to create an alternate way (A Centrally Sponsored Scheme) of providing funding to a larger number of institutions and channelize fund through a body that ensures cohesive and integrated planning at the state level. Such a solution eminent management sense since it is almost impossible for any central agency to deal with 35000 odd institutions on a one- on- one basis. "Given the pitiable condition, wide reach of the state university system and limitations of the UGC, there is a strong need for a strategic intervention for the improvement of access, equity and quality in Indian higher education, that focuses on state universities and state institutions through a special centrally sponsored scheme in a mission mode. RUSA proposes a new centrally sponsored scheme for higher education which will spread over two plan periods (XII and XIII) and will focus on state higher educational institutions,".

RUSA will have a completely new approach towards funding higher education in state universities; it is based on key principles of performance-based funding, incentivizing well performing institutions and decision-making through clearly defined norms, which will establish and rely upon a management information system to gather the essential information from institutions.

Eligibility for Funding Under Rusa

In order to be eligible for funding under RUSA, states will have to fulfil certain prerequisites. These include the creation of a State Higher Education Council, creation of accreditation agencies, preparation of the state perspective plans, commitment of certain stipulated share of funds towards RUSA, academic, sectoral and institutional governance reforms, filling faculty positions etc. Under the scheme, an initial amount will be provided to the State government to prepare them for complying with these a-priori requirements.

Once eligible for funding under RUSA, after meeting the prerequisite commitments, the States will receive funds on the basis of achievements and outcomes. The yardstick for deciding the quantum of funds for the states and institution comprise the norms that reflect the performance in key result areas (access, equity and excellence). The State plans will capture the current position of the states and institutions with respect to these indicators, as well as the targets that need to be achieved. The State Higher Education Council will undertake this process of planning, execution and evaluation, in addition to other monitoring and capacity building functions.

Some of the Highlights of RUSA

Some important provisions of RUSA are highlighted here in order to give awareness to all concerned. Certainly, RUSA can prove to be a boon for the states which are unable to implement the updated modern infrastructure and other essential items for up-gradation of higher education systems due to shortage of fund. RUSA will have a completely new approach towards funding higher education in state universities and colleges. It is based on key principles of performance-based funding, incentivising well performing institutions and decision making through clearly defined norms, which will establish and rely upon a management information system to gather the essential information from institutions. Higher education needs to be viewed as a long-term social investment for the promotion of economic growth, cultural development, social cohesion, equity and justice. The globalisation era has necessitated inculcation of competitive spirit at all levels. This can be achieved only by bringing quality of higher standards to every sphere of work. Therefore, the quality of higher education has become a major concern today.

RUSA will aim to provide greater autonomy to universities as well as colleges and have a sharper focus on equity-based development and improvement in teaching-learning quality and research. It will be a new flagship scheme of the Government of India after successful implementations of SSA and RMSA in the primary and secondary levels of education respectively for overall development of the education system in India to compete with fast global changes. RUSA gives emphasis to ensure adequate availability of quality faculty in all higher educational institutions and ensure capacity building at all levels of employment. It is one of the various goals of RUSA. 'Faculty Planning' is one of its strategic focuses of RUSA and recruitment and capacity building of faculty is one of the primary components of RUSA.

Prerequisites of RUSA

Among others, the following are some of the various prerequisites necessary to be taken up prior to the proposed implementation of RUSA in the respective states, failing which a State may not able to get fund under this scheme. Therefore, it becomes much essential to take up immediate action to fulfil these prerequisites from the side of the State Governments.

1. A State Higher Education Council (SHEC) must be set up. This will perform multiple roles such as: strategic planning, monitoring, evaluation etc.
2. The States must make a detailed State Plan of Action in the prescribed format duly keeping in mind the norms and indicators prepared under RUSA. Future allocations of fund would be based on the achievement of the targets and past performance of the States.
3. The State Government must commit 4 per cent of its GSDP for the State Higher Education Sector, if not in the first year of RUSA, but at least within 3 years of RUSA implementation.
4. It is necessary to appoint full time faculty in adequate numbers. Hence, the states must ensure that the faculty positions are filled on a phase-wise manner.
5. If any state has imposed a ban on regular recruitment of faculty, the state must ensure lifting of all bans on recruitment, and requisite proof must be produced.
6. 'Filling faculty positions' is one of the prerequisites for the states to obtain fund under RUSA. Not more than 15 per cent of the faculty positions can remain vacant at

any time in the state. If any state has more than 15 per cent faculty positions remaining vacant by the end of the first year of RUSA, such states may lose the entitlement for any further grants.

7. The appointments made as well as the faculty already appointed must be remunerated according to UGC regulations and latest pay scales as prescribed.
8. The procedural bottlenecks in the recruitment processes must be actively eliminated.
9. Assessment and accreditation in the higher education, through transparent and informed external review process, are the effective means of quality assurance in higher education. Accreditation will be carried out by a recognised agency like NAAC.

Conclusion

There are various other provisions to get adequate funding under RUSA for the overall development of the state higher education system. It can be truly stated that if a State has a strong desire to streamline the higher education system and wants to bring a great positive change to go into the global competition by developing human resources of the state, then we can rely on RUSA. However, accessing fund under RUSA strictly depend on the fulfilment of the various prerequisites mentioned above and the effective utilisation of fund. All efforts of the state must be utilised in order to finish preparation of ground works in time so that adequate free flow of funding will come under RUSA. This will be the only ray of hope for a poor state like Manipur for growing up our human resources as par with the global changes in a rapid pace. Otherwise, our future will remain a grim. We salute the creators of RUSA and at the same time we request all authorities concerned to work on war footing to welcome RUSA in the state. It will be unfortunate for all, if we are unable to get benefits under RUSA due to the negligence of the official machineries of the Higher Education Department of the state.

REFERENCES

Boele, E. B., (2007). *Handbook on Internal Quality Assurance for Conservatoires* (Utrecht, AEC Publications).

Cavanagh, R. R., (1996), 'Formative and Summative Evaluation in the Faculty Peer Review of Teaching', *Innovative Higher Education*, 20, 4, pp. 225-240.

Harvey, L. and Newton, J., (2004), 'Transforming Quality Evaluation', in *Quality in Higher Education*, 10 (2), pp. 149-65.

Harvey, L., (1995), 'Editorial: The quality agenda', *Quality in Higher Education*, 1(1), pp. 5-12.

Malik, D. J., (1996), 'Peer Review of Teaching: External Review of Course Content', *Innovative Higher Education*, 20, 4, 277-286.

Rashtriya Uchchatar Shiksha Abhiyan: National Higher Education Mission, (2013); Ministry of Human Resource Development in Association with Tata Institute of Social Sciences.

Rashtriya Ucchatar Shiksha Abhiyan (RUSA) draft document retrieved at www.mhrd.gov.in on 15.08.13.

Index

T

U

V

W

Y

*****